Values in Higher Education Teaching

Values in Higher Education Teaching explores the way in which teaching, research, learning and higher education are a values enterprise and that an exploration of values is necessary to work out the full purpose of a higher education to guide practices and help academics understand academic work. Values inform thinking and actions and although this is well recognized, values are seldom brought to the forefront of inquiries as practices in higher education are developed. This book argues that by putting values firmly on the agenda of those who teach, work and learn in higher education, the academic profession can open up new spaces for value conversations and potentially transform the way in which they practice.

Values in Higher Education Teaching is key reading for university lecturers, those with responsibility for leadership and management of higher education, and postgraduates studying for higher degrees in higher education.

There are few books that directly address the broad and complex question of values in teaching in higher education, yet at the same time values are widely recognised as permeating all our practices. In this sense, an accepted part of academic life remains in the realm of 'taken for granted' rather than being consciously and explicitly explored and practiced. The book deals with the idea of values in both a philosophical and practical manner. It is based on original research and uses both empirical data and theory to address teaching values in higher education and the current values of the higher education system. It explores what academics have valued historically in teaching and also addresses the major reforms of the last 20 years. Reforms have essentially changed the nature of western higher education but have made little real difference to the outcomes for student learning and society, whereas teaching with values in all subjects has the potential to radically alter student experiences.

Tony Harland is Associate Professor in the Higher Education Development Centre at the University of Otago, New Zealand.

Neil Pickering is Senior Lecturer in Bioethics in the Bioethics Centre at the University of Otago, New Zealand.

Values in Higher Education Teaching

Tony Harland and Neil Pickering

LONDON AND NEW YORK

First edition published 2011
by Routledge
2 Park Square, Milton Park, Abingdon, Oxon, OX14 4RN

Simultaneously published in the USA and Canada
by Routledge
711 Third Avenue, New York, NY 10017

Routledge is an imprint of the Taylor & Francis Group, an informa business

© 2011 Anthony Harland and Neil Pickering

The right of Anthony Harland and Neil Pickering to be identified as authors of this work has been asserted by them in accordance with sections 77 and 78 of the Copyright, Designs and Patents Act 1988.

Typeset in Galliard by
Pindar NZ, Auckland, New Zealand

All rights reserved. No part of this book may be reprinted or reproduced or utilised in any form or by any electronic, mechanical, or other means, now known or hereafter invented, including photocopying and recording, or in any information storage or retrieval system, without permission in writing from the publishers.

British Library Cataloguing in Publication Data
A catalogue record for this book is available from the British Library

Library of Congress Cataloging-in-Publication Data
Harland, Tony, 1955-
Values in higher education teaching / Tony Harland and Neil Pickering.
  p. cm.
  Includes bibliographical references.
  1. College teachers—Training of—Case studies. 2. Universities and colleges—Faculty—Case studies. 3. Education, Higher—Case studies. 4. Curriculum enrichment—Case studies. I. Pickering, Neil. II. Title.
  LB1738.H27 2011
  378'.014—dc22   2010013454

ISBN13: 978-0-415-58921-5 (hbk)
ISBN13: 978-0-415-58922-2 (pbk)
ISBN13: 978-0-203-84200-3 (ebk)

Contents

Acknowledgements   vii
Foreword   ix

Introduction   1

1 Values   9
  What are values? 9
  Values in teaching 13
  Values in higher education 14
  Conclusion 16
  Values narrative: 'Eddie' 17

2 Understanding values in practice   25
  What's worth knowing? 26
  What's worth learning? 28
  Valuing academic practice 35
  Values narrative: 'East of Kinshasa' 37

3 Teaching values   41
  What's worth teaching? 41
  Six challenges for the values teacher 50
  Values narrative: 'An old teacher, an old friend' 55

4 Valuing higher education   63
  New values for old 63
  A variety of purposes 64
  Shifting (or shifty?) values 65
  Values narrative: 'No more than an image' 71

5 Foundational values   85
The public academic 85
Capitulation and resistance 88
Values narrative: 'Lucy's story' 92

Conclusion   99
Values narrative: 'The goodbye letters' 103

A note on the methodology of narrative inquiry   115
A methodological argument for using narratives 116
What our respondents thought 119

References   121
Index   125

Acknowledgements

First, we would like to thank the six academics who agreed to take part in this research and for generously giving so much of their time to the project. Mary McLaughlin, a graduate of English Literature, provided research assistance. Her patience, enthusiasm, insight and criticism were invaluable. Mary used her skills well on the narrative 'The Goodbye Letters'.

We would also like to thank both Ron Barnett and Stephen Rowland who at various times during the project provided mentoring, good conversation and thoughtful advice.

This research would not have been possible without the generous support of the University of Otago's Higher Education Development Centre and Bioethics Centre. We would also like to acknowledge the financial support of the University, who provided funding through a Research into University Teaching Grant.

Foreword

Professor Stephen Rowland, Institute of Education, University of London, UK

Values in Higher Education Teaching is timely. Recent concerns on a global scale – such as the financial crisis, global warming and water shortages – are reminders that serious attention needs to be given to values in society. If higher education is to contribute to solving such problems, then it needs to consider the values that students gain from the experience of higher education. The values of higher education are often reflected in branding slogans, mission statements and political rhetoric, but are rarely given serious consideration in university policy or practice. Nor are they central in an approach to quality that emphasizes technique, training and measurement rather than virtue, insight or judgement.

But giving values their proper place is no easy task. Most of us even find it difficult to express clearly what we mean by values. An academic's account of their values as a teacher is likely to be brief, banal and bland. Furthermore, they are often at odds with what actually happens in practice.

Progress in the development of values is unlikely to be made by creating definitions and classifications. Harland and Pickering's insight is to realize that the best way to understand (and perhaps change) our values is through the stories in which they are expressed. The core of *Values in Higher Education Teaching* is a series of stories, or 'semi-fictional' accounts, which are a consequence of careful qualitative and collaborative research with university teachers. The impact of these stories is to show how the ordinary life of the academic is imbued with values at every stage, rather than to promote or present a particular set of values. Harland and Pickering leave it for the reader to interpret the ambiguities and uncertainties about values that are expressed in these stories.

In this way, *Values in Higher Education Teaching* enables the university teacher to explore their own values. While the authors argue in defence of a broadly liberal education tradition, their concern is not so much to preserve (or return to) such a tradition as to enable the reader to develop their own judgements and insights about the values that underlie (or might underlie) work with students and colleagues.

When I started reading the book I thought that my values as a university teacher were important. By the time I had finished, I had begun to understand how they may be articulated in the most everyday experience of academic work. That is a position from which it is possible to critique and change oneself, and therefore contribute to change in students and the society they will inhabit. Only if the academic community is able to do this is it likely to make an important contribution to society and the resolution of its problems.

Introduction

> I asked my first history professor in the university, a very famous scholar, whether the picture he gave us of George Washington did not have the effect of making us despise our regime. 'Not at all' he said, 'it doesn't depend on individuals but on having good democratic values.' To which I rejoined, 'But you just showed us that Washington was only using those values to further the class interests of the Virginia squirearchy.' He got angry, and that was the end of it. He was comforted by the gentle assurance that the values of democracy are part of the movement of history and did not require his elucidation or defense. He could carry on his historical studies with the moral certitude that they would lead to greater openness and hence more democracy. The lessons of fascism and the vulnerability of democracy, which we had all just experienced, had no effect on him.
>
> (Allan Bloom, 1987, p. 29)

This book is an inquiry into values in higher education. It has been written in response to a belief that those who graduate from our universities and institutions of higher learning have to take a large measure of responsibility for dealing with the complex problems the world currently faces, partly because educated people seem to have caused most of the problems in the first place and partly because society invests heavily in higher education with the hope of achieving a better future. If higher education wants to play a part in shaping this future, the sector will need to change the way it thinks about its purposes and how it can meet its responsibilities to society. To make this change is a question of values.

Although higher education is a values-laden enterprise, values themselves are seldom spoken about and in the context of teaching, value conversations have largely vanished from the contemporary institution (Macfarlane, 2004). We argue that although values are necessarily the driving force behind all our thinking and that they are lived out day to day in our practices, making them prominent in academic life presents us with great difficulties. Values are difficult to express, often remain hidden in our thoughts and are liable to be overlooked while we get on with the daily business of research and teaching. It also seems that today's university lecturer no longer reflects the radical of old but routinely conforms within an orthodox and fairly docile academic community. Yet, values thinking and action (radical or not) are a means to an improved higher education.

Also of concern is that good educational ideas have been lost or marginalized simply because it has become too difficult to defend many value positions, either for ourselves or in our communities. Even if the majority agree with a value, it is not a case of 'the good will survive'. The 'good' may simply drift off, or be squeezed out of the everyday concerns of a busy academic life. To counter this drift, we contend that there is a need to learn how to articulate a variety of value positions that can guide academic practice. This articulation requires a self-critical teacher, a 'self-critical academic community' and an attempt to live our values in our work (Barnett, 2000).

This book is primarily aimed at the university academic who wishes to learn more about their teaching and the context for this activity. We propose that professional learning and development should include an understanding of how teaching is valued and how to teach values. In undertaking such a task the teacher will need to redirect some of their efforts from learning about teaching subjects to learning about teaching values. Furthermore, because practice is situated within a particular value context, they will also require an appreciation of the contemporary values of the university and the educational services it provides for society. In other words, the idea of valuing higher education. As such, we set out to engage the teacher in a debate about the values and purposes of teaching and of higher education.

Our work is empirical and we collaborated for a little over a year with six academics from different universities in New Zealand (NZ) while each of them considered the question of values in their practices. We reasoned that teaching values is a complicated task and so researching the subject would also have its challenges. Many ideas around the concept do not seem readily accessible to rationale thought or expression and may also be closely linked to feelings or personal and professional identities. We had preliminary conversations with academic colleagues about how they understood values and concluded that the more conventional qualitative or quantitative research methods on their own were unlikely to fully capture the experiences of values teaching. During our initial conversations, colleagues often responded by telling a story to help explain the complexity of their thoughts and on this basis we decided our research would be better served by using a mixed methodology that was based on mainstream qualitative methods and narrative inquiry.

So, we set out to gather stories about values in teaching from lecturers in six disciplinary areas. All could be described as mid-career academics and each worked in a major research-led institution. However, their personal stories are historically located and cover events in their lives as they unfolded in many different parts of the world. We used a variety of methods to record their experiences including conversation, collecting written reflections, correspondence and a series of tape-recorded interviews over the research period. From this data a theory of teaching values was developed which we present in two ways in this book. First, we have a series of chapters based on themes that emerged from the inquiry and second, we recount the stories of the lecturers by way of semi-fictional values narratives. These narratives reflect the complexity of values and how they can be played out in different situations in academic life.

This conceptual structure was borrowed from Jake Ryan and Charles Sackrey's *Strangers in Paradise: Academics from the Working Class* (1984). In their work, the authors provide a thesis followed by a collection of personal essays written by academic collaborators. Similarly, we offer a theoretical distillation of our data and some of the possible ways of understanding values in teaching and higher education and these chapters are interwoven with a series of personal accounts of values teaching. In total we present six short stories which:

- are about values
- are set in situations in which values are implicit
- show values in action, in the actions and reactions of the characters.

These values narratives illustrate how different teachers thought about their work and lives and how they brought values into their own classrooms. Each brief sketch has a certain depth, ambiguity and challenge that we hope will encourage the reader to reflect on their own teaching as they share the successes and struggles of the academics in the stories. Although semi-fictional, each story accurately represents the experiences of the storyteller and in much of the writing we use the academic's exact words. In the more representational stories we remain true to the academics experiences and nothing has been included without their final editing and approval.

For those interested in research methodology, the final chapter of this book gives an account of the narrative research process and the ontological and epistemological reasoning that underpins this. This chapter includes reflective comments about narrative research from our respondents.

Chapter 1: Values

We all live our lives through values, trying to make good choices as we go along. Our abilities in this respect are not innate and much depends on our experiences and how we learn to make decisions and act on them. Our central argument is that values influence the way we see the world and how we operate in it, and in this sense, nothing is 'value free'. We are not concerned here specifically with morals or providing students with a 'correct' set of values. We do, however, argue that every choice a teacher or student makes is informed by their values and they need to become more aware of these in their decisions. However, we reject the relativistic view in which values are seen as 'merely' subjective because they depend entirely on personal preferences. Higher education does have a foundation of values related to such matters as truth, evidence, honesty and so on. To some degree alumni share a common heritage of values, yet some will be able to navigate this values world more easily than others. Relativism and foundationalism are not alternatives, yet to reject such a dualistic position requires some flexibility as we move within and between two seemingly opposed philosophical views on the meaning of values.

For those privileged to attend a university, their capacity to recognize and make good choices is certainly influenced by their experiences. A teacher only needs to take a careful look at students when they arrive and three or four years later when they leave. Students are changed in many ways and these changes reflect their developing values which are, in part, shaped by their involvement in teaching and learning. When they enter the world at large after graduation, students carry with them certain values but must also have the capacity to make new decisions as they take their place in a society; a society over which they will gradually have greater influence as they become older and more experienced. Knowledge and skills are not enough by themselves for an educational philosophy. What seems to be called for is an understanding of the ontological dimension of higher education's purposes that includes questions about the values a university education should represent. The challenge for the university teacher is to work out how values and valuing are taught and learned. The academics who did this as part of our research all saw their teaching change for the better.

Chapter 2: Understanding values in practice

We propose that learning to teach in higher education is a question of values and that this is just as important for the beginning teacher as the expert with many years of service. Teaching needs to be orientated through a clear understanding of values for education and the values students will learn and take away with them. Society today is characterized by rapid change and development and there is a desperate need for privileged educated people to start dealing with the problems we face. We suggest that only with a strong sense of values might students leave university and make a difference in the world and only then will we be able to hold our heads up as 'higher' educators. The current situation seems to lean much more towards a narrowing value position, namely that of providing students with systematic knowledge and practical and analytical skills that will enable them to compete in the world for personal economic gain.

We would also suggest that if a teacher, course team or an institution works out the wide-ranging and full purposes of a higher education, then the question of what a student should learn is likely to include valuing in conjunction with the traditional focus on declarative knowledge and the more recent emphasis on instrumental skills. We are not suggesting a course in ethics or focusing on the ethical dimension to each subject (although this may be a good option). A cursory glance at any mission statement or course document shows they are replete with a range of values, however, these are typically embedded as subtext rather than being explicit and seldom address the subject of values and valuing directly.

Neither are we suggesting indoctrination with a set of values: 'think like me' seems to more closely reflect the current agenda of the state and business but academics and students need to be independent critical thinkers who feel confident to take a critical stance in the world. And such critique should also be for or against the idea of the university, or its values or even the idea of critical thinking itself. Nothing should be off the agenda. We argue that it is a key function of higher education and university teaching to produce wise citizens who are willing to confront and understand their own values, to develop these and to have the intellectual and emotional resource to be able to challenge the values of others. In doing so, the university provides a route to a better future.

However, values and valuing are not easy concepts. To attempt a values conversation usually opens a can of worms. It is difficult enough to be clear about the meaning of something as foundational as 'critical thinking' but to define (and assess?) a 'value' or 'valuing' is more problematic and raises many challenges. Do we, for example, ask students to be 'truthful' or is this just an accepted idea in our academic culture? Could we ever insist a student 'cares' about someone else's learning? Can we ever believe a value such as 'caring' is attainable and how might we know if we have achieved this? Are there values outside of an academic's authority and responsibility? Many difficult questions are raised when values are a concern but academics are seldom prepared to share their thoughts and enter dialogue with others. Articulating different ideas about the values and purposes of higher education commonly carries risk and even isolation within academic communities. The academic who dares to think differently is often labelled nonconformist or cast as a troublemaker.

Chapter 3: Teaching values

Yet academics do have a prime responsibility for teaching values whether they like it or not. We make a case that if learning values is an inevitable consequence of teaching then the academic may as well come to terms with this and make some careful decisions about values teaching rather than let it happen by chance. Toni Morrison (2000) reminds us of this when she wrote: 'What I think and do is already inscribed on my teaching, my work. And so it should be. We teach values by having them'.

The 'chance route', however, does not seem to have a hope in improving our understanding of values, especially in the new mass higher education systems where values questions have become crucial. Because contemporary higher education and society are characterized by constant change, academics would do well to consider systematically exploring the notion of learning to teach values and how they might go about this, perhaps using their disciplinary research skills to become a type of 'values researcher' in the process. It is becoming more common for university teachers to examine their own practices for professional learning and values should be a central consideration of any inquiry. It is far from clear, however, if this change would be welcomed across the academy and it might be seen as just one more task in a pressured academic life. Would academics accept that learning 'values knowledge' is as fundamental to a higher education as learning systematic knowledge?

Our research showed that a good starting point for the teacher is thinking about their personal and professional values as a foundation of the aims for a higher education. If one then accepts that values and valuing can be taught there would need to be explicit recognition that this is part of an academic's responsibility. There are, however, practical steps an academic can take with respect to research and teaching. For example, we often make an ethical choice in what research we choose to do and in whom we work for. In the public university we may not feel comfortable accepting grant income from military sources or doing research for a private company. We have similar choices to make in teaching and remain relatively free to select not only the subject content but, in many instances, how this should be taught. However, once teaching is established it can become routine and there is often little time or incentive for major change. Any reevaluation of practice needs a particular set of conditions and these tend to come around when we are either designing a new course or overhauling an old one. It is here that we can pose the sorts of questions that we may not normally ask and in this chapter we examine inquiry courses and tutorial work as particular spaces suited to embedding values and valuing and exploring what this might mean to learning and teaching.

Chapter 4: Valuing higher education

The values we hold explicitly or tacitly, and those we enact, are influenced by our past experiences and the contemporary situations in which we teach. Higher education provides many different services for society which are unified through a broad range of academic values. Values are an unavoidable result of experiencing university life and therefore a responsibility of the institution and its community. They are a result of an education because to educate is necessarily to pass on a set of possibilities and expectations that are selected on value grounds. They are a responsibility because all such possibilities and expectations, and their implicit values base, have some impact on society. Hence, to understand what is to 'count' as a value, how values are learned and taught, what values are required in learning and teaching and how values attach to disciplines and to knowledge more generally, it is necessary for the teacher and student to come to terms with the purposes and social roles of higher education.

The Western liberal universities of today have traditionally been recognized as an educational site for 'instilling' values, yet modern institutions have experienced great change over the past 30 years or so and there are certain ideas and practices that are now either less clear or that no longer seem to have such a prominent place in the lives of academics and students. These include our understanding of the shared values of academic life and the recognition of the values of an institution. What we seem to require is a clearer understanding of the limits or boundaries of a teacher's responsibility towards the students who are entrusted to them for a few years of their early adult lives. All aspects of higher education are replete with values, are never value-neutral and we are always teaching values and valuing whether we want to or not. So let's not leave values learning as an unintended consequence of teaching.

In this chapter we set the context for valuing higher education against the current neoliberal political and economic reforms that started in the late 1970s. These reforms were important to the six academics in the study and as mid-career teachers they had first-hand experience of the changing context of higher education. Neoliberalism focuses on the delivery of an efficient and cost-effective educational service as a 'product' for a range of 'clients'. Governments, particularly in NZ, the UK and Australia, assumed more control over the public universities to ensure the sector transformed into a mass system and, at the same time, that it became less reliant on public funding and more dependent on both private income and user pays. These complex changes have shifted older values and the academic community has not yet come to terms with what this has done to the more traditional liberal educational ideals that have been foundational to research, teaching and service. What has become clear is that academics are no longer the trusted professionals of old and are now managed more closely using the neoliberal technology of accountability. This adjustment drives academics to be competitive individuals while institutions compete with each other for resources and prestige. The replacement of autonomy with accountability and community with individualism has altered how academics and students experience higher education, what is prioritized and what is valued in academic life.

Chapter 5: Foundational values

One key change seems to have been the gradual demise of the public academic, whose allegiances have shifted more towards the discipline and whatever activity is specified by the state or other influential stakeholder. The clearest example for academics in NZ and the UK is that they are now publicly accountable (and highly rewarded) for the quality of their research and this is where many concentrate their efforts, especially when there is no equivalent reward for teaching or service to counteract this. Accountability and reward of one element of practice coupled with intense pressure to perform ensures clear choices are made between activities, even when the academic genuinely values other parts of practice. Some activities gradually become marginalized as practice changes and values compete with each other as 'more or less' reasonable. However, what is still emerging is the full impact of the recent reforms on the quality of the teaching and research, and the consequences for the public academic.

It may seem that academics have uncritically surrendered their academic freedom as they continue to be driven down a path towards economic activity, market-driven ideology and more state control. Yet ironically, because the ultimate goal for neoliberalism is the privatization of the public universities, government may eventually have to relinquish control and leave everything to the market and business. As we creep towards this position, academics must take some of the blame. There are a few voices that speak out against the new direction but academics have not successfully resisted any of the reforms. Academia's values have shifted much more towards providing an education that will equip students to be good economic citizens with transferable skills that allow flexibility and free movement of labour. Many commentators on higher education have sent out a warning to the sector but they have either been ignored or the universities are relatively powerless to resist the new ideologies. One might also suspect an embarrassed silence as the more liberal messages about higher education's purposes and values no longer seem to be taken as seriously or influence those who teach in or shape the sector.

Yet data showed that when the academics in this study were asked to reflect on values their concerns and questions always had a liberal educational focus, and that becoming more aware and critical of these values made a positive difference to their teaching. This outcome points to a foundation for a higher education and the prospect that values in higher education teaching would make a difference to students' abilities to be explicit about and enact the values for which they stand. If the student of values chooses to make a stand for a better world then the success of higher education will come from the prospect of the continuous addition of value-aware graduates to wider society.

Chapter 1

Values

Working towards a clear understanding of values and valuing is a complicated business. The difficulty seems to be most acute when we think of all our thoughts and actions being imbued with values, and that even to believe in such a position is itself a value decision. Then, because we know that values can change and be learned, the teacher who explicitly includes values in their practice has to resolve the problem of the values they want for themselves and their students (and of course this is also a value decision). To do this the teacher needs to go beyond thinking of values as an expression of personal beliefs and begin to think of valuing as a practical and systematic activity. Values with all their theoretical and practical complexity then become an essential dimension of academic work that a teacher can strive to gain more insight into. In this chapter we will argue that the process of thinking about values and what it means to be a values-teacher will lead to a more reflexive practice that can provide a critical perspective to inform personal theories of higher education, research, teaching and academic life.

What are values?

To put it simply, valuing is about choices. We evaluate as we make decisions about what we do and how we live, and under normal circumstances our thinking and actions express or reflect our values. In turn, our thinking creates the values of the world and, with respect to the focus of this book, the values of teaching and higher education.

There has been considerable argument as to whether the construction of the world reflects only the values humans put out there, or whether anything out there has a value independently of how we decide to value it. But whichever approach we take to this broad question, it is reasonable to think of higher education as a values-enterprise with everything we do, as teachers and learners, being value-driven. This includes the choices we make in what we teach, how we teach, what we select for our research, how we conduct ourselves and how we organize our activities.

We would extend that claim even to the concepts that might normally be thought of or agreed to be 'value-free' (such as theories, evidence and so forth) as these are chosen and used by individuals. Objects and ideas may be recognized as being of 'high quality' or be seen as 'worthwhile' or 'desirable'. As such they provide motives for action. Values therefore become the underlying rationale for the driving force of individuals. If valuing is characteristic of what it means to be human then our values define us in some way and teaching them requires an understanding of their nature and also some effort to keep values at the forefront of our thinking.

However, constantly reflecting on values could be quite disabling and most values become less prominent in our thinking as time passes. Yet when reminded or asked or challenged, we can say that certain objects, thoughts and actions have more value than others. We can describe the values in the different properties of these objects and actions (honest, intelligent, elegant, caring and so on) and as such can recognize a good essay or a remarkable lecture. Yet our judgements about values and their properties will not necessarily be stable and may change over time. Somehow we integrate changing values in our everyday living without needing to have these explicit or well theorized. Elbaz (1992) has suggested that values in general are typically not open to immediate conscious inspection. We generally just 'know' and leave ourselves free for thinking about 'other' more pressing decisions (which, in our argument, is still value-based).

Although all valuing (or value decision making) has validity for the individual, we don't wish to suggest a position where 'anything goes' or that one person's valuing is as good as another's. Some value decisions are simply better and within our communities and social groups we all know this intuitively, and there can be much agreement. For example, although it may be difficult to choose between, say, happiness and rationality, it would be easier to make a choice between slavery and freedom or truth and deceit. When we argue that a value should be more widely held this may give the impression that individual preferences or diversity among individuals are not respected. However, although valuing will be relative to the individual this is always mediated by interpersonal experiences in the social world, for example, through debate. Furthermore, 'respecting diversity' is a value that should also be open to challenge. It could be argued, for example, that if diversity promotes division among people, rather than harmony, it might not be a good value position to hold.

What values are shared and by whom will reflect people's experiences. Many of those who have had the privilege of a higher education will no doubt have many values in common and it is likely that most university lecturers would, for example, agree that critical thinking is a shared value of university life and of teaching and learning. If this idea of commonly held values has validity, then the implication is that not all valuing can be reduced to individual preferences.

So if we believe that some values are better than others and that somehow values can be shared, then the temptation is to look for a foundation for this idea. Such an argument might be termed 'foundationalist' and it counters the 'relativist' stance that all values are relative and depend on who you are. In contrast, the foundationalist idea depends on a 'real-world' view – a view that the source of the value is outside humans and is discoverable. Yet neither the foundationalist nor relativist positions seem to adequately describe either the way in which values appear to work or the complex situations of academic life. This point is well illustrated in all the stories about teaching in this book.

Although we feel the need to reject a dualistic position of foundationalism versus relativism, or a factual world in opposition to a values world, we recognize that we do not have access to an adequate theory that sits outside of these concepts or embraces them both. People are tempted to work within a rigid division between 'objective' ideas or foundational beliefs on the one hand, and 'subjective' or relativistic on the other. But both may direct our responses in different circumstances, and as we negotiate our lives and practices within our communities and society, there will inevitably be times when we call upon either (or both) objective facts and subjective feelings, even as we reject such a false separation. However, the choices that are made may need to be justified and from time to time we will have to try and articulate or negotiate a value position. Because of this, we require an awareness of our values and such an idea sits quite happily as part of the critical traditions of higher education.

An example of practice that seems to transcend a dualistic theory of values comes from the educator, Jean McNiff. She would clearly like a more caring and rational society and in this context she talks about her own values in teaching:

> My values are always those of the other's best interest, where I am concerned to develop the latent potential in each and every one of my clients. We live in a pluralistic society, and I must ensure that each person maintains her integrity to develop according to her own individual potential – always with the provision that she will act in the other's best interest.
> (McNiff, 1996, p. 106)

McNiff appeals to both a values pluralism, which doesn't seek to define individual potential but rather facilitate it, and to a shared and limiting value in the pursuit of personal potential. Both modes of thought co-exist and it shows the interdependence of the two seemingly opposing philosophies. It would probably make no sense for McNiff to frame her ideas as foundationalist without relativism. Her logic is embedded and integrated in her view of the world and it is interesting that she chose 'acting in the other's best interest' as a foundation that also serves to get round possible objections to the relativistic ideas in the first part of her statement. Collier (1993) also supports the idea that values are dispositions towards an activity that need an obligation dimension.

In contrast to McNiff, we met academics in our preliminary inquiries who believed that values teaching was not their business or that we should not be influencing student's values. A typical response was that it is not values but disciplinary knowledge that needs to be taught in higher education. Such a view may stem from the difficulties the teacher faces when they try to come to terms with the value concept. It is so much safer to stick with various forms of subject knowledge even though the values of the discipline have shaped this. Academics may have already been convinced that what is most important in their work is their subject and many seem to spend much of their time ensuring the next generation understands this.

A major problem with teaching values is that we often only become aware of them when they are not shared or they are denied us, and because we are constantly reminded of this experience it adds a negative dimension that feeds into our disposition towards values. How we think about values teaching will be affected by how we understand the concept of values and these views will be influenced by our experiences of their use and misuse in human discourse and personal interactions.

Values often arise in practice, such as the practice of a discipline. The values and valuing of a discipline or other social subgroup can be seen as based in that discipline and can be challenged on this ground. Challenge is necessary and can be positive, but we also experience this in a negative way. This feeling may arise when values are criticized or dismissed as 'subjective opinion' and we cannot always defend ourselves on the basis of rational thought and argument. Someone's values can even be acknowledged and dismissed at the same time because value judgements may be seen as either an inferior way of thinking or as something private to the individual; 'you are entitled to your view' followed by the dismissive comment 'but it's just a value judgement' (or something similar). Such arguments can easily close down discussion and are a commonly used tool for both the subordination of ideas and the control of people. Ideas can be more easily rejected if they are constructed as based on a value judgement rather than 'the facts' or a numerical justification. In these situations values may be denigrated because facts can be more precisely rendered and their source more easily traced, while values may be less choate and less specifiable. We are taught to use facts first and in a modern Western society there is high value placed on objective evidence-based knowledge. Yet when others dismiss our values they are trying to replace them with their own and they may be either unaware of this or convinced that theirs are better, perhaps more rationale, and also immune from counter-challenge.

Some values can also be seen as ideological, particularly if they are of a political or religious nature. An ideology is a collective and comprehensive set of ideas and beliefs that are adopted by individuals or communities, and higher education has its own ideologies. Often the assumptions underpinning ideologies go unchallenged but when an individual's personal philosophy does not sit well within an ideological position, they may be motivated to critique and challenge the dominant view. Ideology often has a negative connotation of bias or being untrue, yet bias is inevitable as people act on deep-seated beliefs and assumptions about how the world really is. These ideologies are part of each of us and in academia we teach our values and, in this ideological sense, indoctrinate our students, whether or not we are conscious of doing so. We agree, however, with Barnett (1990) that although ideology is endemic to much of our thinking it is not necessarily an inversion of truth:

Ideology does not therefore imply falsity; but it does imply partiality, reflecting social interest. From the judgement that all thought is potentially ideological, we should not immediately suspect that falsity is ubiquitous.

(Barnett, 1990, p. 88)

Values in teaching

In an early draft of its current teaching plan, our university suggested that we should teach 'knowledge, attitudes and values that really matter'. A statement and direction of this type would not be unusual for an institution of higher education but will be highly problematic for most teachers if taken seriously. The knowledge part of the directive seems straightforward (although knowledge that 'really matters' could complicate things as this is a clear value statement), however, adding the ontological task of teaching attitudes and values (that really matter) to the epistemological task is much more difficult. If values are commonly associated with personal or cultural beliefs or morals, then academics in most fields, perhaps all those outside of philosophy, sociology and ethics, are unlikely to see values as part of their teaching. And even in these subjects values are likely to be investigated and explained rather than taught to the students. Presumably because of this very difficulty, 'attitudes and values' became the 'development of skills and the building of attitudes' in the final draft.

There are several practical explanations as to why academics may not see themselves as having a responsibility for teaching values. First, the main claim to expertise for the job of lecturer is that of research training in a specialist subject. Academics are then employed as teachers without the necessary level of skill or knowledge and must develop these as they teach, learning on the job apprentice-style. Adding the task of reflecting on the values inherent in teaching during this period (rather than teaching them unreflectively by default) presents the novice with the dual problem of coming to terms with the values-construct and thus becoming an inquirer in an area of knowledge that comes across as rather 'philosophical' in nature. Such deeper meanings of practice at this stage are likely to be outside of the teacher's subject expertise, unlikely to be a priority and perhaps of little interest.

A second reason why academics may not see themselves as values teachers is that there is an epistemological barrier from schools of thought based on technical rationality and the doctrine of objective value (or the value of objectivity) that suggests, particularly in science, that some things are true while others are false. Learning about the subject of values is difficult in this context because value knowledge and value thinking is typically seen as subjective, abstract and full of inconsistencies. The complex relationships between values are not easy to unpick or talk about in purely rational or objective terms and our personal understanding of values always has limits.

Yet values are certainly not merely abstract. The meaning of a value (such as intellectual honesty) has to be appreciated in concrete and particular situations. Values are practical and lie at the heart of our personal or shared dedication to and interest in things around us. They are practical when they are seen as the basis of judgements about what is important in life, what is worthwhile, how one might act and ultimately, the quality of something. In these contexts, values guide our decisions and actions that are then tested against the experience of how far we can, in practice, live by them and realize them. They can therefore represent the sum of our experiences or simply reflect the fact that we are for or against an idea.

Third, if academics conceive of values in the narrow moral sense of the term, then they may not agree that they have a role in providing moral education for young adults. If 'values' are taught anywhere, this should take place where it has always been done – at home and in school (see Macfarlane, 2004). In NZ and in many other countries, the national high school curriculum lists a number of values that teachers should encourage students to adopt and it also suggests that these same values should be part of school life and broader society, thus taking a wide cultural and civic view of teaching a particular set of values.

When our ideas have a moral dimension we make decisions about good and bad or right and wrong in terms of the ethical standards we find acceptable. Values then provide guiding principles for conduct, moral codes and moral value-systems. Judgements of good and bad in this ethical or virtues sense are based on fundamental beliefs shared by many teachers. They are often codified and enforced and an illustration from academic practice would be 'honesty', for example, in reporting research results and the absolute rejection of cheating and plagiarism.

Values in higher education

Recognizing the importance of values to human action, it might be reasonable to expect that one of the outcomes of higher education is that a highly educated person will have a highly educated set of values. By this we do not mean a list of dos and don'ts but that the educated person would understand that they can think critically about their own values and that they have the capacity to develop insight into the value decisions they make. In other words, making value judgements about one's own values, perhaps as ethical, moral or ideological choices.

The experience of engaging with values should also drive us beyond our immediate concerns to something bigger, or at least something on a different level. Engagement drives us toward wider statements of fundamentals and when we reflect on values they present us with questions about which values matter more, about how we live our values and how we try to make sense of them. If we placed thought and knowledge in an imaginary hierarchical system, then such meta-thinking about values might be seen as the pinnacle of a higher form of knowledge. Barnett (1990) argues that this is the essence of true higher education. The important point for teachers is that meta-cognitive skills can be turned towards the question of values and practised and refined in the process of disciplinary teaching.

Although we develop our values throughout our lives, university provides a unique experience for students. Their stay is a formative period and is remembered by many as a rite of passage and a time of self-actualization, when they become more autonomous in their learning and thinking. Students refine their values and come to see what values actually mean in a rich and complex environment and they must make decisions about many things, including answering seemingly infinitely complex questions about how to live. When it comes to teaching, we only touch on part of the student experience and this mainly focuses on the learning environments we create and share as we teach our subjects. Nevertheless, these environments provide us with an opportunity for helping students learn about values, and if the idea that values are going to be learned regardless of the teacher's intention (because values are expressed in all we say and do) is accepted, then we have a responsibility towards understanding our own values, how we live them and how students understand and learn from them. After all, students will go out into the world when they leave university and they have the potential to make a difference, one way or another. Students need to learn how to make their choices as they develop their values and we need to help them with great care. Our young adults come to us with unique experiences that should be respected but it is the business of the university to help them change and develop their values. If we want a higher education that leaves no one out then we need to indoctrinate students with certain values and at the same time understand and be open to the values of individuals. These are not alternatives.

Because values and valuing are learned then it is reasonable to assume that they can be taught. The first thing a learner requires is a way of thinking about values that the teacher can facilitate, perhaps explicitly embedded in a 'topic' or more implicitly as part of the 'processes' of teaching and their relations with students. The potential for values teaching must lie in every aspect of the learning environment and it is worth considering that academics tend to share many values about practice and knowledge; there are codes of academic behaviour, epistemological ideas about truth and, in some societies, the freedom to pursue knowledge and express ideas. Non-conformity to group norms is also a value more tolerated in academia than elsewhere.

Our research suggested that there is little acknowledgement among academics that professional life itself is uncertain and often contradictory and that decisions and choices on how to negotiate this necessarily end up being a question of values. Academics are supposed to be disinterested truth-seekers and the professionals to whom society turns when it tries to find certainty, and hence the idea that the search for objective knowledge will sort out the problems and complexity of all our lives. But what sort of knowledge and expertise is this? If it is knowledge that rejects the values that create it, then its own worth may be called into question. And if there are academics who believe their work inhabits a value-free part of the world, they are likely to maintain such a façade and no doubt resist engaging with the values dimension of their work. Values and values teaching will be left outside of their area of expertise and, at best, will be someone else's concern.

These issues are not esoteric and they do matter. They matter every time the teacher walks into a classroom because every interaction that takes place reflects the individual's and institution's values. And if our students are learning values from us, then it is incumbent upon us to find a way of thinking and talking about them. As academics, it is not common to ask questions about our own values or talk about how we teach them, yet the research for this book has shown that it is possible to get a high level of engagement through simply raising awareness of the issues and encouraging a personal journey of reflecting on values teaching. This outcome has shown that values can become an integral part of practice without the teacher necessarily having to have a fully worked-out theory or understanding. We suggest that the concept of the 'scholar' is founded on a person having a sense of what they value and it would be difficult to think of someone described as 'scholarly' as not having a commitment to a clear set of values that are both articulated and practised. The scholar has academic integrity reflected in the way in which they think and act in the world, and would recognize values as both a product of and a motive behind a higher education. As such, values become part of the purposes of teaching.

Conclusion

Understanding the idea of values has consequences for the academic and their practices as researcher, teacher and provider of services to society. Although some teachers may choose to help others learn about right or wrong, all will teach values through their everyday activities and interactions with students. This will happen whether they are aware of it or not and the teacher may sometimes become a reluctant role model. As a consequence of the ubiquitous nature of values, the knowledge project of the university is value-laden. Thinking about these ideas, however abstract they may seem, creates a new awareness of the purposes of a higher education. There are two values questions that every academic should be able to answer, while recognizing that getting a good answer may take a lifetime of inquiry. These are:

1. What is the purpose of a higher education?
2. How do I achieve this in my research and teaching?

Values narrative: 'Eddie'

Eddie crosses the road, ignoring the red figure. He edges his way past the slow walkers, dodges round the ones coming the other way. Sorry! (hitting someone with his bag stuffed with marked essays). He skips across the grass and into the café, which isn't really a café, just where people sit and have a smoke outside the building. There's no one there yet – too early. He joins the little group waiting by the lifts. No one there he knows. Good, as he doesn't feel much like talking. He gets a lift with a couple of students. They push the button, and the lift rattles upwards. The students are quiet too; perhaps they're getting essays back? They get out first and go right, Eddie goes left.

Having put his bag down in his room, and extracted Melissa's essay, Eddie makes his way down the corridor, sees Dory's office door is ajar, and knocks on it. 'Come in,' a deepish voice says.

'Hi, Dory. Got a moment?' Dory always has, so it isn't necessary to ask, but Eddie's serious tone catches his attention. Dory likes Eddie – his enthusiasm and happy outlook (despite some unhappy events recently at home). Odd that he should teach such dark subjects – 'Evil and the Image', 'The End of life'. Popular too – both Eddie and the subjects, that is. Probably – certainly – some connection.

'Take a look at this, Dory,' says Eddie. A stapled set of five or six sheets. Eddie's tone suggests there's something seriously wrong. While Dory reads, working his lips, Eddie looks out of the window.

'Hmm.' Dory hands the essay back.

'It's pasted, lock stock and barrel, Prof. I stuck a seven-word string in Google and I got the whole bloody thing second hit.' Eddie needs to express his exasperation, his anger, his disappointment (he's shaking). 'The whole bloody thing, word for word, every reference, every footnote, even the stupid acknowledgements. I can't believe that last bit. The acknowledgements!' Later they laugh about it.

How to handle it is the question. As Dory says. That's the question. But what does it mean, first? 'It means,' says Zelma in the staff coffee break, 'that we can't trust our students – even the best ones (the apparently best ones).' Zelma's comments don't relate to Melissa in particular: and Eddie isn't about to share this particular one with the whole staff room. In any case, Zelma and Eddie have always disagreed about this sort of thing. Zelma is 'Inspector Z'. 'We (the faculty) are the guardians of the standards, the guarantors of justice.'

18 Values

Some student stays up every night in his lonely flat for a month reading, note-taking, writing, and produces garbage; another one does bugger all and then downloads his answer and gets an A. Our job, says Inspector Z, is to catch the miscreant. Blah blah.

It's the wrecking of the joint project, learning together – that's what it is, not that police nonsense, thinks Eddie. That's what it means. Staring at the desk and unable to do anything else but think about it. That's why we need trust – both ways. But, goodness, the times I've tested the trust of my students – I mean, teaching them when I was hardly a chapter ahead . . . Then along comes this sort of stuff. I mean how can I treat them as 'fellow learners' when someone pulls this sort of stunt. There is a knock at the door.

'Come in.' It's Sandy, Eddie's teaching assistant. She looks solemn; sits down, head bowed. After a while she can't fight back the tears. 'I can't do it, he ruins my classes.' Not for the first time, she's struggling with her work. Eddie took on an assistant because his classes got too big for one person to teach and tute. Sandy's a PhD student. And frankly, she's right, he – Paul – does ruin classes. He just takes over – won't shut up, always has a story about his own life or his family which just fits (in his eyes). It's exhausting in the big class – but at least there you can keep things moving ('well, we must get to the next slide . . .'). In Sandy's small tutorial group where discussion is what matters . . . What does one say?

Eddie has a line – but it's not just a line. Though sometimes – today would be a good example – he feels like it's just spin – but it isn't. It's about affirming the Other, with the big 'O'. And Paul is very much big 'O' material. But he's human – of course – with a life, needs and so forth. Frankly, Paul has problems. He is difficult – 'high maintenance' as they say these days. Well, that sums it up rather well, actually. Sandy is rather high maintenance too, mind, but she knows when to stop – you don't avert your gaze or skulk in the coffee room. But when we stop affirming Others – mayhem, destruction, torture.

That's not just melodrama either, because Eddie has seen it, first hand: a grim teacher was Cambodia.

The phone rings and the university receptionist says: 'It's Melissa Tancred – shall I put her through?'

'Hello, Dr Kent, it's Melissa from your class. I was wanting to come and talk to you about next year.' Ah-ha: Eddie quotes Blackadder internally. 'About which courses to do.'

'Well, Melissa – yes, we must think about that one.' Assuming you haven't been chucked out in the meantime. Eddie hesitates. Say something now? Say nothing now? 'Err – I wonder if you could come in and see me about your last essay? Today? Yes, soon as possible – well . . . yes, this afternoon would be fine.' Not. Could be a somewhat dry-mouthed lunch – Eddie always goes dry in the mouth when he's nervous.

'Are you OK, Eddie?' asks Sandy, perhaps noticing his slight distraction as he puts the phone down. Not really. Eddie says: 'Look, I'll have a word with Paul – I've got to see him anyway – and we've got a staff meeting to discuss issues like this later this morning. OK?' Well, not really, either. But Sandy goes, passing by Dory just outside in the corridor as she does, who comes in and pulls the door shut behind him. Must be serious – most discussions are open door around here.

He pulls up an easy chair, and sits himself in it. He wants to know what Eddie is going to do about the essay.

'She just rang,' says Eddie. 'Wants to talk about her courses for next year.'

'Hmm.'

'I've arranged to see her after lunch.'

They both know it's a big one. Plagiarism is rumoured to be rife, the press is snuffling around, the internet is the source of much of it, and the implications are huge.

But, says Dory, carefully, she's the only one we know of. There may be others we don't know of, he admits, but we can't assume the worst. We mustn't, for the sake of the other students. And, of course, we need to know more. Why? What's going on? No accusations, no verdicts, see what she has to say – let her go first. Inside Eddie can feel his guts relaxing, his juices beginning to flow again. Trust Dory to come up with something practical! Yes, thinks Eddie, that's the way: today is not judgement day.

'And there are avenues too, Eddie, processes – it's not all down to you.' Of course – Dory's hit it on the head – Eddie has been feeling it was all down to him. But there are channels, committees, appeals – it's sort of comforting. Time for the staff meeting.

After stuff about the timetable and research leave, the meeting finally gets around to the subject of Paul. 'How the hell did he get in to the course, anyway?' demands Dr Wilkinson. 'His academic record is lousy.' 'Falling standards,' chimes in Inspector Z. 'The answer is to weed them out right at the start.'

'That's not the answer here, though, Zelma,' says Dory, reasonably.

'He's a nutter,' says Dr Wilkinson. Eddie reddens and starts to respond – because that's the kind of talk – worse, the kind of thinking – that leads to disaster. Eddie wants to be reasonable but everything he hates and was brought up to hate is in that sentence. What's different is to be contained by law or medicine or something which can label it and make it alien – a cage of some sort, which keeps the wild animals in. Eddie's passion comes from images of his childhood and his parents. His mum in particular did a lot of work with the mentally ill at a time when the big asylums were shutting down and these pale, slightly confused and challenging people were let out into the sunlight. Some of them found their way into the backyard one afternoon, and Eddie still remembers them, and his mother making them cups of tea and his father talking for hours with this one guy about some cosmological thought he'd had. A lot of them, apparently, also found their way onto campuses. Dr Wilkinson isn't fazed by Eddie's tirade, and doesn't take it personally. And Eddie himself, having vented, is fairly quickly relaxed again, a bit shamefaced, and apologizes. He likes Wilkinson, who's a straight talker, but can take it as well as give it. What to do, again, is the question. Any suggestions?

How about lunch?

Yes, good idea, a quickish one as Eddie has a tutorial group at 2. They troop down to the nearest café. 'You know,' says Dory, 'I remember when lunch was always at the old Pig and Porcupine. We used to go and have a beer with the students, sometimes a couple, and then we'd come back to the department, and give our lectures.'

Wilkinson nods. 'I could tell you one or two stories along those lines,' he says, winking at Eddie.

'Wouldn't get away with that these days,' says Eddie. All three shake their heads and sip their cappuccinos.

Eddie makes his way back to the department for the tutorial group. They're in the lift as he sprints in, and hold the door for him. 'Thanks.' An hour or so later, he emerges from the seminar room feeling better. That was a good session. Interactive, good questions, good discussion. Five or six keen students, all of whom know one another and know Eddie, and who are comfortable to speak. Well, it's a good group that particular one. Not for the first time Eddie reflects on the amount over the years he's got from students. How was Sandy's group, he wonders. Coming round the corner, there's someone waiting outside his office. His mouth goes dry. But it's not Melissa, or Paul, but a potential new student who wants to talk about the courses for next year.

Eddie welcomes him into the office and talks to him a bit about a new course he's offering next year on the Technological Imperative – If you can do it, you should do it. It's a big issue for Eddie, who has seen what humans are capable of. 'The big question in this course,' says Eddie, paraphrasing the blurb, 'is "what does it mean to be human?"'. Actually that's the big question in almost all the courses I run.' And all those I ever have run, he adds silently. The student seems interested, and collects various pieces of literature from Eddie before heading off.

Melissa's essay is still on his desk where he left it after speaking with Dory this morning. After gazing at it for a minute or two, Eddie turns to his computer to check his emails. There's a knock at the door. A breath. 'Come in.' It's Sandy again, and Eddie is relieved. 'How'd it go, Sandy, this afternoon?'

'Fine,' says Sandy, who seems much brighter. 'Was anything said at the staff meeting? About Paul?'

'We did discuss him,' says Eddie. Not that there were any great ideas on the subject.

'My problem,' says Sandy, 'is the other students, really. I mean, I feel I'm short-changing them all the time, because I spend my whole time trying to deal with him.'

'Have they complained?' asks Eddie.

'Not yet, well, not to me. Have they said anything to you?' Eddie reassures her there've been no complaints – not about Sandy at any rate. 'They've spoken to me about him from time to time, just passing comments, you know. And by the way, they recognize when you're trying to do things to manage a difficult situation – and appreciate it.'

'Do they?' Sandy seems further brightened by this. 'Are you going to talk to him, then?'

'Yes, I'll do that,' says Eddie, 'but I think the problem isn't going to go away. Is there any way you can divert attention on to the other students? I mean, get them more involved.' Sandy muses for a moment. Yes, she thinks there are things she can do there. Eddie feels he has achieved something at any rate, as Sandy leaves with a few practical things to try out.

Back to the emails: mostly spam, as usual. Must get that spam thing set up to screen them out. There's another knock.

Melissa Tancred comes in. Eddie reflects that he has enjoyed his previous conversations with her. He likes chatting with students about their essays, and he has found her receptive, intelligent.

'Have a seat, Melissa.' Eddie lets her get sat down, but he holds back for a while before starting. 'Melissa – I've just been reading your last essay.' He holds it up for her. 'And, well, I'm . . . well, basically, Melissa – can you explain something for me? I mean, basically, I found the exact same essay on the net.'

There's a blank stare. Then the tears . . .

When she's gone, Eddie hurries down the corridor to find Dory, but his door's shut (a sure sign he's out). Fredericka, his secretary, confirms that he's lecturing. 'He'll be back about 5,' she says, looking at the wall clock.

Eddie returns to his office, and pulls the door to. Then he goes over to the window to look out. His talk with Melissa has left him confused. He isn't sure what his role is in this case. The technological imperative: if it's on the internet, download it. Come to think of it, that's how his own children use the internet for their homework. Cutting and pasting stuff. They get good marks too. But if Melissa has cheated then doesn't he owe scholarship something? Honesty, rigour, all the things that he believes in and lives by. And what does he owe Melissa? And the other students, what does he owe them? There are no winners in such situations, Eddie thinks. He's glad when he hears Dory's voice down the corridor.

'Ah!' says Dory, as Eddie arrives at his door. 'Go in, sit ye down.' He shuts the door behind them.

'Well, there's an explanation – time running out, pressure, family. And then there's the "this is the first time" and "this is the last time" stuff.'

'She's got a family? Didn't know that. How did you leave it?'

'I said I'd have to talk to you about it, and that we'd see where we went from there.'

Dory nods. 'And where do you want it to go?' he asks. Eddie hadn't thought about that one. Where did he want it to go? Away, basically. Forget it. Pretend it didn't happen. Set new essay title and new deadline. Return to the Garden of Eden. Paradise Regained.

'It doesn't need to be anybody's business but yours and hers, if you don't want it to be,' says Dory.

'It may be enough for her,' says Eddie, 'I mean, it's given her one hell of a fright.'

'Or she's thinking "Got away with it again",' says Dory.

'Hmm. But I can't believe that, Prof. I mean, it can't be that she's been turning in essays like this one for three years.'

'How would we know, if she was?' asks Dory.

Eddie blanches at the thought of it. And more so at the thought of going back and looking at all those essays again to see if . . . Eddie is looking out of the window again as he entertains these stray thoughts. 'Why did you get into teaching, Dory?' he asks.

'To change things, I think,' says Dory. 'That was a time of revaluing things. Challenging power structures and the old order. Exciting times. Questioning, looking at other explanations than the accepted ones. Opening minds.'

'You know, Prof, I had a really good tutorial today. And another student coming up to ask about the new course for next year . . .'

So, thinks Dory after Eddie's gone, he's still got that energy. He's got balance in his outlook. I like that. We'll sleep on this essay business. He packs his case slowly, wondering vaguely whether he needs the laptop tonight. No, not tonight. The Professors Delaney are coming to dinner and they'll want to be up late. But on the other hand, he hasn't got any meetings 'til the afternoon, so tomorrow morning he could stay at home and work. Rather too many calls on one's time at the office. After a moment's more hesitation, he packs the laptop.

Chapter 2

Understanding values in practice

Four key themes emerged from our inquiry into values that provide an alternative starting point for learning to teach. These are presented here in propositional form:

1. That universities have a values foundation but contemporary reforms are modifying this for both the teacher and the learner.
2. That teaching values creates a new way of thinking about knowledge and academic practice.
3. That in order to teach values to others we first need to examine and explain our own values.
4. That learning to teach is still an amateur activity.

Understanding the broader foundational values of higher education is key to understanding what we teach and how and why we go about this activity, and this will be examined in more detail in Chapter 4. At this point it is sufficient to note that today's higher education is becoming more complex and characterized by constant challenges and value incursions. Teaching takes place within this broader values context that shapes academic identity, how the academic thinks about teaching and what is permissible in practice. The biggest challenge for the academic has come from the move to mass higher education, driven by both the desire for economies of scale and the drive for 'added value' as the sector seeks to produce more and more educated workers for the new knowledge economies. Students are taught in increasingly large classes and what was once a rather intimate activity has become more depersonalized. At the same time, especially in the research-intensive universities, teaching has been effectively separated from its research foundation and is increasingly devalued as a secondary activity. To ensure quality in this new low-value teaching culture, academics are held personally accountable to a host of stakeholders, which has a tendency to drive teaching into safe spaces with both risk and innovation replaced by unadventurous curricula.

The new ways compete with established practices and older values, and when systems are in a state of flux, the teacher has a more difficult task in pinning down the purposes of a higher education. In this chapter we argue that they should, however, carefully determine what they value for their practices and what they are trying to achieve for student learning. We make a case that putting values into teaching practice requires a new epistemology for learning that is much more conscious of its ontological roots. In being more conscious of what we value, we become more aware of how our beliefs inform our teaching.

The chapter is divided into the following sections:

1. What's worth knowing? This section examines the broad implications of a higher education in today's societies and how certain values might guide teaching.
2. What's worth learning? What's worth learning is primarily about university lecturers learning to teach and the place of values in this process.
3. Valuing academic practice. We conclude the chapter by providing a model for professional learning that shows a relationship between ontology and teaching method.

What's worth knowing?

'What's worth knowing?' is the title of Chapter 5 of Neil Postman and Charles Weingartner's 'Teaching as a Subversive Activity' (Postman and Weingartner, 1969). Their book is a commentary on the condition of high school education in the US in the 1960s. The authors' main proposition is that the world we live in is in trouble and that many of the complex problems that societies have to deal with have been created by so-called educated people. Education has therefore, in their opinion, failed us (so far), yet it also remains the only means by which we can deal with the challenges ahead. However, they argue that for this to be successful we have to look for fresh approaches to teaching and create a new type of education that focuses less on the dissemination of factual information. In their quest they ask 'What's worth knowing?' which is a values question that reaches to the heart of teaching and it is as relevant today as it was in 1969.

'What's worth knowing?' should be asked by all those who teach in higher education and it has even more potential here than in high school for two reasons. First, there is still a large degree of individual freedom and choice in what we teach and second, academics usually prioritize the knowledge they want to research. Knowledge creation and knowledge dissemination are thus closely intertwined and how we decide to use this unique situation for a new type of education requires careful thought about the learning experience we create for our students. It is also important to remember that the university system has had great successes in the past and that there are many examples to be found of what might be called 'quality' experiences that go right to the heart of higher learning. Students can still receive an excellent education and teachers can provide experiences that stay with students for the rest of their lives. These events tend to be closely linked to liberal educational values that include such ideas as critical thinking, close teacher-student relationships and teaching that is securely in touch with the processes of learning.

So when we talk about developing an alternative starting point for learning to teach, we acknowledge that there are already ways of going about our work that are extremely worthwhile, however, we argue that these are not common across the university. At the same time, teachers are aware of different possibilities and choices for teaching and despite the increasing restrictions on academic life, individuals and groups still have enough freedom to work out what they value in teaching and learning, and the opportunity to put this into practice.

University academics are first and foremost inquirers in a subject area that gives them knowledge and their claims to expertise. How to pass this knowledge on seems to be the normal starting point for teaching. There are decisions to be made about what parts of a subject are relevant, at what stage complexity should be introduced and the best way to present information. Once this is sorted, there are decisions to be made about learning itself and how students can be developed as subject learners in the field. A crude way of illustrating the idea of developing learners is to say that if we want to help students become, say, highly tuned critical thinkers, then this is likely to happen most effectively when the teacher values the concept enough to make it a central concern for their teaching and student learning. So, this university teacher can 'add value' to the student experience by aiming for their students to become critical as well as knowledgeable.

What might happen next seems to be more complicated. We can use our subject to help develop good learners, but for what purpose? It is here that values come more to the foreground. Although we have argued that values are foundational to all that happens in academic life, we also make the point that they are mostly implicit and unspoken. When the teacher is pushed into dealing with questions that require a value judgement, they know from experience that there is seldom an easy answer or resolution. The teacher who endeavours to work out their educational purposes lives with uncertainty and because of this, it is often easier to ignore this dimension of practice. If our students graduate with good knowledge and thinking abilities, have we not done enough? Yet without considering the broader purposes for student learning, any answer to 'what's worth knowing?' simply lacks relevance in the wider world and we are in danger of remaining firmly in the grip of older information-rich educational paradigms of the type that Postman and Weingartner criticize. The knowledge project should be ultimately judged by how our students make a stand for what they believe to be a better world.

Universities are open to a wide range of values so a foundation for teaching practice is not always clear. The recent emphasis on values such as 'economic gain' does not just drive out other values but creates new ones. To attempt to exclude new values closes doors, leads to problems of justification and leaves the university open to the charge of resisting change or even of reversion to elitism. However, a foundation of values seems to be what we need as it gives an institution and a teacher both a 'bottom line' and 'aspiration' for practice. This foundation appears to be essential to any inquiry into the value of a higher education. Here is a short list of ideas that have embodied the Western university traditions:

Freedom of speech
Critical thinking
Tolerance
Respect
Knowledge
Truth
Creativity
Democracy.

Such foundational concepts are embedded in most visionary institutional documents but in the practice of teaching they may be unrecognized, ignored or undermined as contemporary academic life becomes stretched thinly and reshaped ideologically. Busy academics may not take much notice of value statements and some may simply be content (or even grateful?) to have the opportunity to be able to pass on some factual information and knowledge. In the research intensive universities of the type reflected in our study, academics are constantly pulled away from teaching and a substantial portion of this activity is done by temporary 'teaching only' staff, postgraduates or senior students, or there are attempts to replace some teaching tasks with learning technologies. Furthermore, many new courses are designed to meet current economic imperatives and there is pressure to prioritize certain values such as knowledge relevant to employment and transferable skills training (Macfarlane, 2004).

> The pedagogical relationship becomes economized. 'What is it worth?' comes to rival 'Is it worth it?'
>
> (Barnett, 2003, p. 123)

Yet in all situations teachers seldom publicly declare their values and, as a consequence, many university academics don't appear to stand for anything beyond disciplinary knowledge. To put values into teaching, individuals will have to step back and take a close look at what is happening in society and the higher education sector, work out what their educational purposes are, and then get down to answering the question 'what's worth knowing?'

What's worth learning?

It remains an interesting fact that the only experience and qualification needed to teach in a university is the mastery of a subject and the ability to research and develop new knowledge in that field. Because of this situation, university teaching differs from research and from the work of most other professions. In the practice of law or medicine, we would not let someone be an autonomous practitioner without many years of education, training, practical experience and close supervision. In the university we take researchers who may never have taught before and let them lose on the minds of others (usually young adults) with full autonomy and seemingly without considering that this might not be a good idea. Of course some will be 'natural' teachers from day one, others may learn quickly through trial and error as they go, and many now take postgraduate teaching courses during their early years. However, is it appropriate if the new academic learns their craft at the expense of students' learning? Is it appropriate for an academic to go through their career unaware of their full potential as an educator?

'What's worth learning?' becomes a question for the academic and it concerns how they learn to teach. Here we look at the circumstances of professional learning and then suggest a possible starting point for an inquiry into learning how to teach values. In this context the university teacher aims first to be both knowledgeable and explicit about their values, and what this might mean for their practice.

Most university academics gradually learn to teach through trial and error as they reflect on their experiences, but this is certain to be limited if it is done privately. Postgraduate courses are now offered for new teachers in most universities and they can have a major impact on learning but unless compulsory (which itself may present a cultural barrier to learning), they tend to attract low numbers and often teachers on the fringes of mainstream practice. Furthermore, present day programmes are typically based, for practical reasons, on a rather narrow version of educational psychology learning principles without addressing many of the other social, political and philosophical dimensions of teaching that are an inevitable part of academic life. Postgraduate courses therefore tend to be dominated by certain values to the exclusion of others. However, they do open up a space for different value conversations.

Despite postgraduate courses and the collective efforts of the academic development community, we are left with individuals who need convincing that putting some effort into learning to teach is worth it. They can be driven into the position of learner in early career by the need for survival in the classroom, and later when they are forced to examine their teaching, for example, if they are required to produce evidence of teaching quality for promotion purposes. Being desperate or compelled, however, is unlikely to have the same impact as being motivated and free to learn.

The way in which an academic chooses to develop their teaching involves personal decisions and judgements about practical tasks but there are good reasons why values considerations need to be central to all processes of professional learning. We have already made the point that an academic teaches values whether or not they want to or are aware of it, and this indirect or 'unconscious' condition seems to be, perhaps paradoxically, the most powerful method for passing on values and changing a student's value position. In the interactional space of teaching, students pick up the values of the discipline as they construct knowledge and learn to 'think like a zoologist' (or historian or doctor or lawyer, etc.). They learn values around say, critique, from the way in which the teacher deals with controversial knowledge. They see what is acceptable on a personal level by the way in which they are treated and by what they are required to do or by what their teacher allows them to 'get away with'. There are also explicit values in every curriculum and some, such as the way teachers assess students, are powerful determinants of learning. However, it can be quite disturbing to think that implicit values are found in everything we say and do, and that our actions, conscious or not, may influence aspects of student learning. It is also pertinent to remember that the novice teacher also learns values from observing those who are more experienced (Van Manen, 1995).

It seems unlikely that most lecturers would think about practice in terms of a concept of values (unless of course values is their subject). Our study showed that this did not happen in the normal course of work but that it was possible for each teacher to look back and describe practice situations where values came more into the foreground. Respondents tended to recall events that were important to them or their students and situations that required personal or professional decisions to be made in order to resolve an issue. There were moments in every day when the teacher was called on to make sense of their values, make value decisions and act upon them, even though they may not have been thinking in terms of values. Our respondents recognized that their values would be noted by students who they saw as learning how to play a part in their new professional community by finding out what 'the other' thinks and does and then working out the best way to think and act. Yet because values seem to operate for the most part at the intuitive or tacit level it will be possible for any teacher to go about their daily business without necessarily having to consider values or how they impact on students, and much of professional practice must be based on unquestioned experience and routine.

Although the teacher can get a sense of values when these are called into focus, our argument for professional learning is to make values the object of inquiry outside of these events. An intention to engage with values thinking brings them more or less to the foreground and this habit can be learned, practised and refined. Learning about teaching values takes careful thought but most importantly it requires a reason for doing it (either forced by a situation or through personal choice) and then a way of dealing with the practical implications of new thoughts and ideas. The narratives in this volume illustrate this process and in the extreme a strong value position can seem quite radical or even dangerous, in the sense that the teacher may step outside of the accepted norms of academia (a particularly good illustration of this point is found in 'No more than an image' in Chapter 4 of this book).

What may put the learner off from considering engaging with the idea of values is that the concept is rather abstract for everyday use. Values are something that we know we have, that we can hold dearly, and that we recognize as shaping our actions and our views of the world. However, articulating such ideas is a challenge and our respondents needed the process of taking part in the research project to encourage their reflections. Yet even this did not seem enough and after a year of thinking about values, both from a theoretical perspective and in relation to examples from practice, it became clear to us that value questions require a very precise and relevant focus if we are to really gain by giving them our attention. For example, the values of higher education and teaching appear rather distant from the practical realities of the classroom and lecture theatre, and we found that it was specific events that occurred in teaching that had the most potential to bring values into focus.

Much of university teaching seems to operate with instinct or what 'feels' like the correct thing to do at the time. One respondent suggested that most of us are never truly tested on our values and as a consequence we may be living our lives as a sort of fiction. Of course this is not much of a problem until our values are questioned or denied. Then the individual needs to find out how deeply their values are held or whether or not they need to change. Donald Schön has argued that we hold theories for our behaviour:

> These theories of action, as we have called them, include values, strategies and underlying assumptions that inform an individuals' pattern of interpersonal behavior.
>
> (1987, p. 255)

He then goes on to say that these theories operate at two levels, the espoused level that we use to justify our actions, and theories in use, that are implicit in our actions with others. Schön argues that we can't easily explain our theories in use and that what we say and what we do may be incongruent. Espoused theories explain the way we would like to see the world, but they do not always describe how we act.

Learning, however, can also be exceedingly laborious, not to mention hazardous, if people rely solely on the effects of their own actions to inform them what to do. Fortunately, much of human behavior is learned observationally through modelling; 'from observing others one forms an idea of how new behaviors are performed, and on later occasions this coded information serves as a guide for action' (Bandura, 1977, p. 22). If we do develop an espoused theory of teaching values, we would probably attempt to explain this in terms of strategies and assumptions because values themselves would be too abstract to represent our experiences to others.

There are, however, fundamental problems with learning about values through observing others or reflection on practice. The key difficulties lie in the fact that thinking about values is an act of valuing itself and also that there are several values characteristics that can hinder us. One's own values:

- are not always obvious to oneself
- tend to change over time
- are not always acted upon
- can't be measured (which has implications for assessment, teaching choices and learning)
- can be in a state of tension with one another
- can't be transmitted because they are in us and in the production of what we do
- can be received by others in a different way from that in which we have intended.

To make any statement about values requires certain values of the person making it and active control of one's thinking about this is both difficult to do and consuming for the mind. Although Schön (1987) asks for reflection in action (in other words thinking about what we are doing while we are doing it), we are suggesting that for thinking about values this is more difficult because of the circuitous routes and circular logic of all values thinking. Values thinking seems to be characterized by uncertainty and recognition that there are only temporary resolutions to a question. The values teacher needs to try and step back to bring values into focus, but this promises no solution and it is possible to end up in a blind alley of abstraction and experience both confusion and frustration. For the teacher who is sure that values consist of nothing more than subjective concepts or personal opinions, there may be little hope of learning more about values in teaching.

Part of the difficulty in engaging with the idea of values comes from the academic traditions of Western thought. At one level the university imagines that it operates in a rational, 'value-free' and objective manner but objectivity is simply another strong academic value. No subjects or disciplines are value-free, although we try to think that this might be the case, especially in the sciences, and values do not sit easily within an ideologically objective academy. The university tries to accommodate all views in its 'value-free environment', though there is always a bottom line to what is acceptable in academic life. Our respondents gave numerous examples to illustrate this foundation, including such issues as academic dishonesty and plagiarism.

So values are the foundation of our actions and what motivates us, and they describe the things that really matter. Thus no one operates in a truly objective or value-free manner. The key question is whether or not pedagogy is consciously directed by values and then consciously directed towards values. Our respondents seemed to do this by directing their thoughts and reflections towards one central issue of practice at a time and then engaging in a focused inquiry about specific values in context. If such an observation holds more widely, then for thinking about values in practice the best way forward will be through small incremental steps, while accepting that values themselves are likely to be altered at the same time.

Another difficulty for learning about values in teaching is that they are often personal in nature and emotional attachment may make them harder to discuss with others. In addition, once we declare our values publicly our actions are more easily judged. Teachers probably don't often talk explicitly about their values with their colleagues and this position was reflected by the study. There is also a complexity to the language needed to develop a useful dialogue with others who may not be like-minded so it can be quite difficult talking about values, even when we accept that challenge and contestation is the lifeblood of academic discourse. When a question of values is challenged it can be very threatening, unpleasant and often seen as a personal attack. Furthermore, recognizing and labelling something as 'merely' a value judgement is an easy and culturally acceptable way of undercutting someone's argument. We did, however, have examples from our research in which individuals collaborated with trusted colleagues to enable values conversations to take place. To be truly useful, this also required a special critical relationship because we can run the risk of learning very little from those who think like us or agree with our thoughts and ideas, rather than criticizing them when necessary.

In contrast to values teaching by modelling and default, learning to teach values directly and systematically can give us a lot more control and may feel more measured, even if it is argued that it could be less effective for student learning. In deciding to teach a specific value the teacher will also reflect on and change their tacit knowledge by trying to put this into words and make it more explicit (Polanyi, 1966). Most importantly, a specific value can be made part of a judgement about what's worth knowing. If a teacher is not sure about the scope of their values, the values of university teaching or the values they might decide to teach, then a good place to start is the statements in institutional documents. This approach might seem shallow to some but anyone without grounding in this area of knowledge has to start somewhere and a fresh or critical look at these documents is one way of getting a hold on values. If an idea looks interesting the academic who decides to consider it seriously will start a long journey of discovery as the new value is realized in the complex real-life situations of teaching and learning. Of course there are dangers in such an instrumental point of departure including the difficulty that the values listed in documents will have been carefully selected with alternatives just as carefully excluded. However, there is no harm in beginning here when other strategies are not available. If we examine a few extracts from our own institution's documents as a case-illustration, we suggest that they would not seem out of place in any other Western university. These were accessed at www.otago.ac.nz in 2010. At the institutional level, the University of Otago's Charter has a section on academic values and suggests that these should be concerned with:

1. Defending the principles of academic freedom, open debate and civil discourse.
2. Exposing students to the full range of paradigms, theories and methods at play in a field of inquiry.
3. Learning from the accumulated body of human wisdom, which has established that:
   - knowledge is provisional and open to reinterpretation
   - the university – an institution that is part of and interactive with wider political, economic and cultural forces – is a repository of knowledge, site of critical inquiry and agent of social change
   - critical, creative and ethical inquiry is best served when teachers and students are free to express and examine the societal commitments and biases that influence the production, dissemination and application of knowledge.
4. Respecting the ability of students and teachers to jointly contextualize, critique and compare different approaches and contributions to human knowledge.
5. Evaluating students solely on the basis of their academic performance, and our peers solely on the basis of their contributions to scholarly and creative activity, teaching, university service and the wider public good.

6. And, finally, inspiring and communicating the joy and excitement of intellectual endeavours.

If this list is seen as a set of tasks, then it is quite a challenge for any university teacher, even though each idea may seem relatively uncontentious. If we examine the instruction for teaching in the University of Otago Teaching and Learning Plan we can see a slightly different expression of values in the following extract:

> The University of Otago promotes quality learning through the acquisition of knowledge, the development of skills and the building of attitudes. Quality learning within specific disciplines and across traditional disciplinary boundaries assists learners to apply what they have learned to practical situations now and in the future. Oral and written communication skills and the ability to collaborate effectively are vital.

Here we run into more challenging terrain because the ideas become less specific. One might ask, for example, how the teacher might go about teaching 'attitudes' or 'effective collaboration'. In the same plan there are also expectations specifically related to a type of values thinking:

> The University of Otago expects learners to evaluate and debate the ethical, social and community implications of the knowledge, skills and attitudes they have acquired so that they are informed in their opinions and in their ethical values.

In this guiding statement we are driven towards values, but not just any value. In this case it is those that have an ethical dimension. Later the plan goes into more detail and the university nails its colours to the mast with the following:

> The University seeks to produce graduates who are able to reflect upon and evaluate the ethical and social implications of their knowledge and who are willing to act upon that awareness whatever the ethos of their ultimate employment. The ethical and social values of a university education should transcend the pragmatism of the workplace.

We would stick our necks out at this point and suggest that most academics do nothing more than glance at mission statements and teaching plans. And if they do read them closely, the directives will seldom be seen as a guide to thinking or behaviour. The culture of a university tends to arise out of the capacity of the individual to evaluate it and not the other way round. When enough individuals share values across an institution (for example the value of research-led teaching), then the university culture is identified as strong. However, a university community all too often consists of a collection of individuals or small groups, rather than the broad inclusive 'community of scholars' characteristic of the liberal educational ideal. As a consequence, many value positions find a place and these may or may not match the ideals of the institution. At some point a stand will have to be made on certain values that are deemed central to academic practice, for example, academic integrity and plagiarism (Macfarlane, 2004).

Many academic values that also depend on a dimension of personal character, such as 'integrity' or 'conscience', are less likely to change radically as academics develop their practices. Specific values that are imposed in charters and mission statements, such as 'defending academic freedom' may seem a more appropriate option for learning but they can also be accepted in an instrumental way if they are seen only as functional. Instrumental values are unlikely to last and if they are viewed as a means to an end, it is difficult to get a sense of personal ownership and commitment to such ideas (unless the value is threatened). We end up with incomplete correspondence between academics and their institution with academics being gradually drawn into the values of their closer communities of practice. While they sit outside of the effects of institutional socialization they may miss an opportunity to look at certain values in depth or in broader context.

Although it takes far more than a document to change practice, such statements do reflect a set of values and offer an interesting synthesis. They can provide a starting point for putting values into teaching and guide the teacher who wants to develop thinking in this area. We would conclude that first working out one's values and then attempting to live these in professional life is a foundational task for all who teach in higher education.

Valuing academic practice

Rising to the challenges of teaching values starts with personal inquiry and a commitment to professional learning that includes a consideration of values. We propose that developing an alternative epistemology of teaching requires a methodological turn. The significance of this is that the academic develops a personal theory of teaching to explain their thoughts and actions and recognizes that such a theory is based on how they view knowledge and how their values affect their understanding of this.

Table 2.1

Ontology	Epistemology	Methodology	Method
An account of a world view based on values that inform beliefs	The nature of knowledge, its foundations, scope and validity	The study of teaching and a theory of practice	The techniques and approaches a teacher uses
Informs →	Informs →	Informs →	
Experiences of teaching inform one's methodology, epistemology and ontology			

The concept of ontology in this model represents a person's obligation to the values that inform their preferred choices and how they see and represent the world. Ontology describes their reality. Methodology becomes the principle guiding a study of teaching and the development of personal theories of practice that in turn inform the techniques and methods employed in classrooms, laboratories and lecture theatres. The implication is that the university teacher becomes a 'researcher' of their own practice and that this process starts with considering what is of value. Similar structural ideas can be found in practitioner-action research (Whitehead and McNiff, 2006) and in the theories of the methods of qualitative social research (Grix, 2002). Teaching becomes a subject for research and the university academic can focus their considerable intellect and research skills on this venture. In this model, the first topic in the project is values. The precise focus that we think is necessary for questioning values can come directly from personal experience or from theory. Through this inquiry process we can endeavour to give an account to others of how we influence the quality of our students' learning and then begin to answer some of the bigger questions about the purposes of a higher education and 'what's worth knowing?'

Values narrative: 'East of Kinshasa'

Edward enjoyed sitting out on the verandah in the evening and watching the Kwilu and the river traffic. It was uncomfortably hot and humid, but the ritual of sharing ice-cold ginger beer made things more bearable. He had met John at Oxford and when the letter arrived to say that he was so near, Edward had decided to take a few days off rather than wait until term ended. He was still feeling the pleasure of meeting an old friend and thought of their deep friendship that he knew would last, even though they were so often out of touch.

John: So why did Dimandja get malaria?
Edward: Because he was bitten by a mosquito carrying the malarial parasite.
John: Why did the mosquito bite Dimandja?
Edward: Bad luck.
John: Do you think that Dimandja believes this?
Edward: Probably not. Of course he understands about parasites, but he'd also 'know' that someone must have wished him harm and sent the mosquito to bite him. Perhaps a spirit.
John: So he lives in two worlds. In one science talks of parasites and germs, in the other he listens to the witch doctor?
Edward: In some ways, yes, I guess he does.
John: But some theologians live in two worlds as well?
Edward: Yes, academic study of the Bible opens the danger that you become 'schizophrenic'. The academic side of you treats the Bible as another collection of ancient texts to dissect, while the religious side still reads it as a word from God. For some, the religious side gets diminished.
John: So the suggestion that some chapters of the book of Isaiah were written centuries after Isaiah's time makes the Bible less holy?
Edward: Well some students just reject the scholarly conclusions, or follow the conservative scholars who claim that the whole text of Isaiah was written by Isaiah. They find the ideas I present too threatening.
John: Another case of 'science' against religion?
Edward: In the face of such an either/or presentation, I am looking for another way. I ask them to imagine that the scholarly interpretations are true, and to look at how we might then understand the words. In that case the text comes alive in a different way.
John: You're asking students to be scholars, like you?
Edward: Yes. But for some I just seem to challenge the authority of the text.
John: How does Dimandja cope?
Edward: Better than most! He seems content in a world where the two positions sit alongside one another.
John: If you are not thinking of this in a dualistic sense then you are seeking the middle ground, a compromise.

Edward: Not so much a compromise, as an openness. I feel that these students have every right to reject an academic critique. But at the same time I have to try and discourage them from doing so, or at least to help them understand the reasoning behind the position they dislike. I also try to enable them to integrate their beliefs and their scholarship. I feel that I would be cheating students if I did not make them aware of other ways of seeing the world.
John: How does this 'openness' affect their learning?
Edward: Well, I hope that while we pull the text apart, when we go on to examine it as a whole again, the process adds something. Of course there are always other scholars who come to different conclusions!
John: Who is right?
Edward: There has to be some way in which the text came into being. I do believe in truth. And even ardent postmodernists accept that one thing can be more true than another! We know enough to make intelligent, realistic guesses.
John: Is this a tension between your Christian and academic cultures? Or between Western and African?

On the journey to Kikwit to see John, Edward had thought much about his experiences at Oxford and the start of his academic career in Glasgow and how this contrasted so much with his new life in Africa. The chaotic world outside of the college. A society living on a knife-edge with extreme poverty and an infrastructure falling apart. No reliable water or electricity system with entire districts of the city existing in the dim light of paraffin lamps. The road was safe at the moment although he had been very conscious that last week a bomb had destroyed the post office and damaged the radio station. One person had died.

Edward: When I think back to the culture of my school days there was a rigid system that did not allow for shades of grey. There never appeared to be any doubt about the certainty of knowledge. Science was the queen and 'value judgement' was a negative term.
John: Do Western Christians live with such certainties?
Edward: Of course some will, but others learn to question.
John: What about the Western academic's or the African academic's relationship with knowledge and truth?
Edward: I think that each would understand the nature of truth in different ways. As a teacher, I have realized that I have to justify my beliefs, my interpretations. Then students have the option of arriving at a different conclusion. Rather than simply agree or disagree. It avoids a fight. The 'take it or leave it' position of the Church I grew up in nearly resulted in my leaving for good. If you remember, I went up to Leicester with that intention.
John: I remember it well.

Edward: The right to disagree strikes me as important. It's a significant part of what it means to be human.
John: But how easily can your students disagree with you?
Edward: I say 'this is what I believe and here's why'. Then you open up the possibility for them to come to a different conclusion. Yet you always run up against a point beyond which you can't reason. Where you do simply have to take it or leave it. When you are not going to be capable of convincing somebody else. For example, I believe in a Creator but reasoned argument alone will never convince someone else.
John: Strikes me that you're asking your students to accept the presence of these contradictions. Between faith, and ideas that can be proved?

Edward never saw confusion in Dimandja's eyes. There seemed to be an acceptance without the need to resolve conflict. An acceptance of new ideas without necessarily abandoning old beliefs. In contrast, some of Edward's Western students couldn't live with this sort of duality. There was an underlying cultural thread that assumed the world we seek to explain was largely impersonal or objective. For Dimandja, each glass of water was a gift, saying 'grace' over water was natural to Africans.

Edward: There is a tension in teaching this way, because I am in a particular position of power. In my teaching I try to provide the strength of rigorous thinking while enabling students to retain the things that make us human.
John: Do you try to teach that directly?
Edward: No. Not consciously.
John: There must be many other things you teach in this way too.
Edward: All sorts of things. Simply because of the way I am. I think that what you teach and what you are are internally related. A large part of what I teach is who I am. I think this is why I initially inherited a materialistic view of theology from my own teachers.
John: Were they not also deeply spiritual?
Edward: Yes. I guess it's not that clear-cut. But if you don't communicate this spirituality, then you give the impression that the world is a place where the personal side of things has less importance.
John: Could the personal side of things be seen in terms of indoctrination, rather than education?
Edward: I agree. But without putting one's self into teaching, students might get a good education in terms of knowledge, but might lack wisdom. Wisdom comes from the intersection of different views. Wisdom comes from engagement.

John left the verandah to get Edward another drink. Edward stared at the river and thought about engagement. Everything taught at his English public school had a right answer and pupils had no voice to criticize. However, as a pupil he had quickly learned the art of subversion. There seemed only one choice when you didn't feel like going along with the system. MNC-Lumumba had claimed responsibility for the bomb blasts at the central post office and the Voice of Zaire.

Edward: In my late teens I thought that my church expected me to take the Bible as a textbook on everything. But that did not work. The early chapters of Genesis, for example, have a different order of events in chapters one and two. That they are teaching us the history of life on earth just seemed wrong. It wasn't until I went up to university that I discovered there were other ways of approaching the issue. Ways that were more open, more reasoned. People could take different positions and still talk to each other.

John: As an academic and an authority in your field, you must carry some conception of truth?

Edward: I think Western academics are two-faced about truth! On the one hand, we are so aware of the culturally conditioned nature of what people perceive as true, and of the slippery nature of language obscuring meaning. On the other, we act as if values like tolerance or scepticism were some sort of absolute.

John: Postmodern critiques of metanarratives certainly seem almost polar opposites of what theology has traditionally been about!

Edward: In some ways they are, yet with their understanding that human knowing and human motives are always complex and flawed they could also resonate with Christian understandings of human nature and enterprises as inherently flawed – 'enslaved to Sin' in the traditional language.

John: Pilate's question: 'What is truth?'

Edward: If there is no Truth, you no longer have the grounds to claim that some things are true and that others are false, so you end up pretending that everything is equal, or relative. If there is no such thing as an absolute truth, then teaching is a very unsatisfactory position to be in.

The voice on the Land Rover's radio had put the blame on Libya. The blasts had been 'isolated incidents of urban terrorism', whatever that meant. What sort of new text would this produce? How close to the truth are we ever going to get when the story unravels? Yet when Mobutu controls the media, it's hard to know what to believe. Edward thought that none of it makes sense if you can't pin it down to some sort of truth. Everybody feels that some things are right and some things are wrong, and that some things are good and others bad. A boat facing upriver caught his attention. Was it moving? It was several seconds before he decided.

Chapter 3

Teaching values

This chapter builds on the ideas of self-inquiry and greater ontological understanding, and focuses on what and how we teach. It is divided into two parts:

1. What's worth teaching? Here we consider how lecturers can be more explicit about values and the types of curriculum experiences that are useful for teaching and learning these.
2. Six challenges for the values teacher. From our research we identified six value-problems that teachers face in their work.

What's worth teaching?

Throughout a teacher's career they will come to know about the practical side of teaching while developing knowledge of what can and should be taught. On the one hand, teachers tend to make similar choices because there is something about 'graduateness' that can be understood and broadly defined, and after three or four years at a university students will have many values in common with those who have had a similar experience. On the other hand, each teacher has a lot of freedom in teaching and ideas about what to teach differ between individuals and often change over time. Conscious inspection of teaching can include both the subject of values and values as subject matter.

If 'what's worth teaching?' is accepted as a question of values, then the teacher can start by being explicit about values and align these with their values for a higher education. Such an exercise changes the nature of practice because values begin to compete for new intellectual and practical spaces in teaching and learning situations. What might seem to be rather theoretical ideas can be transformed into knowledge that can be taught directly by inclusion in assigned tasks (e.g. a requirement for evidence-based argument), through the educational process (e.g. provide problem-based tasks to achieve new skills in problem-solving) or by teaching valuing (e.g. including the idea of making values decisions in the curriculum content).

> Lecturers aim at the training of students in the systematic knowledge of selected subject areas and in the related analytical skills . . . The clarification of concepts, the checking of evidence and inferences, the marshalling of evidence into coherent conceptual structures: these powers of intellect are indispensable for the contemporary world . . . Among staff, there is a strong belief in certain values, for precision, for logic and so on.
>
> (Collier, 1993, p. 289)

University teachers tend to teach within a narrow specialized subject within the confines of the boundaries of a discipline and will likely accept culturally determined ideas about disciplinary knowledge in terms of what is necessary for students to learn and how this might be learned. We also suggest that it is not uncommon for a teacher to concentrate their efforts on the processes of learning rather than factual content. However, it seems rare for teachers to explicitly teach values or valuing. Adding this new dimension could give the sector a different foundation for a higher education. One respondent in our study suggested that such an idea could be conceptualized as wisdom: 'the manipulation of facts gave us information and that information was the foundation of knowledge, but that knowledge with an understanding of values would give us wisdom'.

We may partly get round some of the difficulties of teaching values by thinking of this as a process of valu*ing*, just as we teach critical thinking, reasoning or analysing. Then we provide the student with the cognitive tools to understand issues about values and handle ideas that can transcend the discipline, just as critical thinking may not just be a skill related to the disciplinary task at hand. Valuing becomes a process and another layer for consideration in the learning environment. This strategy could also encourage students to question their personal educational experiences as they seek answers about what a higher education means to them as they learn to develop and exercise a capacity for value judgement. For the teacher, being specific about particular values to be included or excluded presents a difficulty, yet without some attempt to do this the question of which values are worth teaching remains theoretical. We have produced the following table as a way of helping academics consider values questions in their teaching.

We are aware that the table only represents a small sample of possible values and that some of the these can easily be shifted between categories or from low to high and *vice versa* in the right circumstances. The dichotomous nature of the table also oversimplifies the nature of values. However, it raises questions about the limits of responsibility, for example:

1. How far down the left-hand column does the teacher go before they feel uneasy about their expertise?
2. How far down the right-hand column does the teacher go before they disagree that a value is low?
3. When does a value-topic become 'not my responsibility'?

Table 3.1

	Education for:	
	High value	*Low value*
Knowledge values	Knowledge Critical thinking Evaluation Originality Creativity Application	Information Repetition Rote learning Spoon feeding
Academic values	Honesty Integrity Fairness Truth Evidence	Cheating Plagiarism Dogma Emotions
Attitudinal values	Caring for others Respecting others	Selfishness Individualism
Public service values	Freedom Democracy Citizenship Social Justice Equality	Oppression Inequality Discrimination

Universities do provide attitudinal and public service values even though higher education's project is often directed by the discipline and subject expertise. If a shift towards values is to be made, then academics will have to consider the broader purposes of a higher education and we know there are opportunities for this because those in the present study showed that a wide range of values decisions were brought into everyday practice. From time to time they had to make complex decisions around educational purposes, both for themselves and their students. When confronted by values problems all put time and effort into understanding them and how they might best respond. This reflective task often required a commitment to reevaluate teaching beliefs and the limits of individual responsibility.

Although our respondents confronted values in all their teaching there was no doubt that certain types of curriculum spaces provided additional opportunities for consciously including values. We suggest that because courses are often regularly evaluated and changed, either radically or incrementally, such exercises provide an opportunity to consider the question of values in our practice.

Course design as a value space

'What's worth teaching?' is dependent on the teacher's values because they decide how they should teach and to a large extent how students should learn. For example, if a teacher values, say, participatory decision making in learning, then they will find a way to build this into their curriculum and it will form a context for learning. Students always learn to think within the context that the teacher provides.

The freedom we have to create unique teaching contexts carries with it a responsibility to design appropriate spaces for learning. Students enter a space on trust because they are seldom sure of what they are letting themselves in for. Most learning experiences in higher education have an element of chance because the student never knows who they are going to meet along the way or exactly what type of experiences they might have. There is very little opportunity for a learner to make genuinely informed decisions about their studies and they tend to take the rough with the smooth. It is often a matter of good luck if a student enjoys a course or meets an academic who teaches in a way that they find valuable for learning.

In planning a course teachers tend to work out the subject content and how best to get this across. Mastery of a body of knowledge within a disciplinary context is foundational, however, this can translate into an experience in which students are subjected to covering and remembering masses of factual information. Mastering knowledge, however, also requires higher order learning skills for understanding and communication. So the teacher adds the higher-order skills of reasoning, synthesis and dissemination of knowledge, and such an experience will hold students in good stead. But knowing a lot about something once in your life, or having the capacity to be a good learner and thinker still does not seem to be enough for a philosophy of higher education. One might ask questions such as: why be a good learner? a learner of what? a learner for whom? and who does this learning serve? These are ultimately values questions about purposes that seldom get asked in educational debate. Carl Rogers and Jerome Freiberg set out their views on the broader purposes of our educational systems:

> [W]e wish to aid the development of our most precious natural resource: the minds and hearts of our children and young people. It is their curiosity, their eagerness to learn, and their ability to make difficult and complex choices that will decide the future of our world
>
> (1994, p. xxi)

In this sense there seems to be a fine but crucial line between having knowledge and being truly knowledgeable and crossing this will require a journey into the world of values. A consideration of values can help the student aim to become a good subject specialist and a good learner, with learning that is embedded in the values of the discipline and applied to the value questions of concern to the individual, higher education and broader society.

So, how do we design a curriculum that allows us to confront and realize such values? For a start the complex process of personal teacher development and changes to teaching practice will require time and commitment and in the research-led institutions of this study, neither were easy to find, mainly because of a pressured working environment in which research was clearly prioritized. Success and other rewards came through this activity and teaching was seen to be undervalued. There are also likely to be academics who simply do not attach importance to teaching and undertake this activity reluctantly, yet even they teach what they value, whether this is passing on factual knowledge, teaching students to work in a group or teaching higher-order learning skills.

Students can learn about values through practicing making values decisions. In this context, what the student does is more important than what the teacher does and so the curriculum should include the rehearsal space necessary for the student to learn through an active process of valuing. One simple way of doing this is to build in experiences that require value decisions. Material is chosen to ensure values are contested in discussion and a typical example would be the pressing ethical implications of a subject. Collier (1993) suggests that 'the critical question will be the extent to which the validity of those values, as experienced by the students, is opened up for debate' (p. 295). Apart from seeking out ethical problems, it is possible to include other value problems in our courses but in doing so we may need to overcome certain objections. First, teaching a specific value that sits outside of established knowledge or academic norms of a discipline is sure to meet resistance from others (fellow teachers and students) and in the end the risk may not be a practical option. For example, it is easy to imagine critical thinking being an educational objective but it is harder to imagine, for many disciplines, a value such as 'caring for others' being listed as a learning outcome in a course document with its associated assessment task. So if we are aiming to put such a value into practice, then we may have to do this in a more subtle way and engineer an outcome without ever being so explicit about it. Such a strategy could leave the teacher open to the charge of being underhanded or deceitful, yet this is likely to be the norm for many teaching and learning situations that will include unarticulated aims and implicit values. This 'hidden curriculum' seems inevitable and, in any case, the full outcomes of an educational experience can't be measured, predicted or even known with any great certainty. Any academic who believes that their written learning outcomes fully and accurately reflect student learning experiences is kidding themselves, even if they have evidence of partial alignment from their assessment tasks. Learning is much broader than we can ever know and values often fall into the category of 'too hard to measure' (like many other worthwhile ideas).

Likewise, colleagues in a teaching team will have limits to the sorts of things that they see as acceptable or that they feel comfortable declaring. Our study showed that individual teachers have to operate within these broader social structures. In some way, what we see as 'normal' or 'acceptable' comes from the common world we share and qualified consensus, and as such, teaching is done in the practical space between foundationalism and relativism. However, there is nothing necessarily rational about the agreements we make, nothing true or false. If there were, then we would simply recapitulate a foundation of values, which clearly does not happen. So, it is what we make of this practical space that counts and we may decide to take radical departures or, conversely, avoid putting ourselves at risk by stepping too far from acceptability.

A further consideration is that we are required to include assessment tasks in our courses and certain values will be much more difficult to assess than others. We may attempt to measure something like critical thinking or be on the lookout for plagiarism but many values for learning would be seen as on the fringes of accepted assessment practices. If we can't measure an outcome objectively or at least agree on standards, there is a tendency for teachers and students to assign it less importance or ignore it for assessment purposes.

Our research showed that if a teacher decides to include explicit values in a course, they also need to work out how to bring tacit values into the open and into words. Teaching explicit values is likely to require an interactive setting in which students and teachers can hone their thoughts and ideas through challenge and affirmation and for some this will be seen as messy or even threatening. Teaching for a value requires some thought around how values might be formed, changed and developed and the teacher will also need to think about how students become aware in the values debate and what impact this experience has on them. Collier (1993) suggests that we need to be conscious of the complex amalgams of perceptions and values that are at work in ourselves and others and that 'We cannot escape the conclusion that a higher education . . . should include a component concerned with the diagnosis of subjective perceptions and value-assumptions' (p. 289).

Despite such challenges for teaching, students come across wonderful teachers and courses as they make their way through higher education. We recognize that values teaching may not be an explicit aim for these educational experiences, however, there are practices that stand out as exceptional in some way, and we can learn from them. Very often they can be identified easily because they are so different to what is going on around them locally, and to what might be representative of the institution more broadly. Our study showed that such events had the following characteristics. They:

- were often private to the teacher and students
- were grounded in the liberal educational traditions of learning
- were required large investment of time and energy for teachers and students
- were had high impact on students
- were typically under threat of compromise or even closure.

Such curriculum experiences were found in all six disciplines we examined and they tended to be the responsibility of the lone academic, more rarely with the help of a small number of others who shared a commitment to a certain kind of education. The 'liberal traditions' included a particular set of values such as helping students become critical thinkers, promoting learning through human engagement, developing a curriculum that supported self-actualization in the learner and teaching that aimed to develop freedom within a community of learners. Furthermore, the student was typically given some opportunity to develop 'disinterested' theoretical reflection by which we understand that learning transcends the utilitarian role of education and mirrors more closely the liberal ideal of knowledge as an end in itself. What strikes an observer about these teaching and learning 'events' is how they contrasted so markedly with 'routine teaching'.

Such exceptional courses must be widespread across higher education because of the many examples that are described in the literature on teaching and learning. They form the basis of claims for teaching awards, are presented at higher education conferences and are shared through online repositories. However, because they often rely on an individual's passion, take time and energy to both develop and maintain and may not be seen as cost effective by a department or institution, they are fragile and typically under threat of modification or closure. If one had to classify these programmes the majority would come under the category of 'inquiry', although thinking of them literally as 'learning through research activity' would also be fairly accurate. In the next two sections we take two curriculum examples of the type found in our study that appear to be advantageous for teaching valuing and values. These are inquiry courses and the tutorial. Both are at once unremarkable, well recognized and accepted in traditional university teaching, and at the same time, neither are well understood, especially by the novice or inexperienced teacher.

Why Inquiry?

Inquiry and the creative impulse seem to be intrinsic to human nature and teachers can harness this to allow it to flourish and develop. Inquiry-type courses provide a complex and challenging environment for students to realize their creativity and such experiences teach values simply because they raise values questions which are inevitable in any authentic inquiry experience. A common illustration of this property is when a student first enters the primary research literature and finds two accounts of the same phenomenon with contradictory outcomes or conclusions, both of which are in peer-reviewed journals and written by established researchers. The student is initially frustrated but, if curious, will be driven to make new types of judgement about the topic, the nature of knowledge, what counts as evidence, the reliability of method, the peer review process and so on.

In this illustration the student has entered the world of the academic. Of course this is a well-recognized path for university teaching and by the time a student is in their final year or becomes a postgraduate, doing research and being 'supervised' rather than being 'taught' structures learning. However, at this later stage education is highly selective and what we are suggesting is that the process should begin from the day students enter university so that we do not risk crushing the learner's internal drive, their curiosity and their creativity, and then gradually and painstakingly try to reconstruct this in our top students-as-researchers. Most universities seem to have a tendency to equate ability with an assumed developmental stage and consequently save their main efforts for teaching higher things at higher levels. They then wonder why some students find it difficult to meet their expectations. Some institutions, such as McMaster University, Canada, have committed to the principle of inquiry courses for all first-year students. Yet the typical first-year experience, outside of a few elite institutions, is still one of attending large classes, didactic teaching, learning the basics and memorizing large quantities of information.

The organization of teaching in each academic year might be based on ideas about capability levels but are seldom founded on the principles of inquiry learning. Beginning students are capable of dealing with inquiry problems and may have experienced a lot of research activity at high school (this position is certainly true for NZ). When they come to university they seem to be quickly socialized into less meaningful ways of learning. One reason for this is historical in that the sector has organized its work this way for a long time (and most academics will have experienced a similar system). Another reason might be that an academic's sense of identity comes largely from disciplinary research and their subject expertise becomes a form of power and authority; their role is to act as a gatekeeper to a world into which only the most interested and very best students will eventually be admitted. Of course academics do have this duty but in this sense they are not educators inviting all students in. Another explanation is that as the academic becomes more expert in their own learning and more aware of the structural ideas of their knowledge and thinking, that they simply become tempted to relocate the end point of this into their students and favour transmission-type teaching and learning strategies. We live in a transmission culture of which the university is a part and 'teaching as telling' seems quite normal.

Whatever the reason for organizing and perpetuating university education in traditional hierarchical stages, we can still consider alternatives. Why not teach first years in the way we teach our PhD students or try and reflect the way we learn? Why set standards for student learning that are different to those of our own? Developing an early habit of inquiry in our students will produce 'good learners' and open up the educative process to values but like any change, it will have a cost. The sheer quantity of information and factual knowledge that students acquire must shrink because there will simply not be the time available to sit and listen and take it all in. Furthermore, although the subject is still foundational to inquiry, the relationship between the knower and what is known changes dramatically. Authentic inquiry also needs a climate of trust because it is usually a messy process of false starts, problem management, compromises and often less than ideal outcomes.

How we assess such a process in undergraduate education also creates a challenge that requires either creative solutions or acceptance that not everything can or should be assessed. The dominant ideology of assessment and evaluation is to seek technical solutions that exploit the qualities of science, but measurement of this sort often separates reason from emotion and the teacher from the student. Objective measurement also seems less convincing for judging inquiry and we would argue that if values and valuing are important aims for learning, reason needs moral choice and both learning and assessment require a close relationship of trust and understanding between teacher and student.

If inquiry is accepted as a way of bringing values into the curriculum then the next challenge for the teacher is how to introduce specific values into the inquiry process. How might a teacher ensure that a student undertaking an inquiry will learn, for example, to evaluate their own learning or show evidence of integrity in their work? And when do the more complex tasks, such as 'recognizing bias' become part of the inquiry process?

The tutorial

In our study, many of the reflections and stories were located in experiences of tutorial teaching. This was a place where values were often brought to the surface and the contested nature of knowledge became central to learning. We believe that we can exploit tutorials in all disciplines for the express purpose of learning values because learning becomes an inquiry made public and experiences are shared.

Of course there are many different types of tutorial although they should all aim to create an intimate social environment. A student may be chosen to read a critique of an essay or research paper while in another a group discussion on a contested topic is used. Whatever experience is planned there is social interaction which plays a key role in learning and development. Students learn from others through discourse that helps them become familiar with the values of the subject, discipline and the learning environment.

The tutorial teacher will try to convince students that the experience will help them become good learners and that to do this requires practice and experience. The tutor can support the student's need to know 'the facts' and develop a good memory, but they can also encourage them to develop the ability to judge these facts, to discern good from bad and right from wrong. Because such a process ultimately requires personal insight, the tutorial can also afford opportunities for helping students develop self-understanding as part of a vision for how they might want to live their lives.

In tutorials, the student observes the tutor closely just as the tutor observes the student. We accept that it is good for a teacher to know learners, what motivates them, how they learn and so on. It is less common to turn this idea around and think of the tutorial as a space for students to learn from the actions and contributions of a teacher. How they interpret these qualities impacts on how they understand their own values. In her reflections on teaching values in university, Toni Morrison writes:

> Through everything I say, write and do, however I may try to stand between, to the side, or over issues of ethics and value when discussion is underway, my position is either known or available to be known.
>
> (Morrison, 2000)

Yet our research showed that students can find the whole process difficult and are quite happy to bypass knowledge uncertainty, contestation and questions of value. Breaking away, even partially, from the powerful culture of authority and transmission is not easy and tutorials can be seen initially by students as having little relevance or value. As they mature as learners they may recognize the need for intellectual tools to criticize and judge but building this capacity in tutorials during the early stages of a university experience can be a challenge for any teacher.

One of our respondents was keen to try and put the learner in a 'safe' tutorial environment in which they were accorded respect and their values acknowledged. Yet when values are critiqued or contested, students are never quite safe. They will often find themselves at odds with the values of others and not all have the same abilities in discussion and argument; when one student succeeds, another may fail. This outcome might seem like a natural state of affairs for the tutorial but tutors are conscious of it and tend to put boundaries and frameworks around what is acceptable in discourse. Students need to decipher these codes and regulate their own behaviour. Tutors may use a disciplinary rationale to make sure tutorials don't stray too far from the central topic and keep students focused on the subject. Yet the student's primary operating mode and the value decisions they make will be influenced by past and present interpersonal experiences: whether or not to engage with a topic, whether or not to speak or listen, how they think a contribution will be received, whether or not they take a risk with a tentative or controversial idea and how they empathize with others (see Rogers and Freiberg, 1994). Students will have a great deal of interest in whether or not they end up feeling affirmation or hurt. Being balanced, fair, open-minded and even-handed in arguments can be very difficult to achieve in the tutorial, especially when someone feels strongly about an issue or when the tutor seeks to introduce a value outside of the dominant academic culture.

What seems to be crucial for inquiry courses, tutorials or any other curriculum experience is to understand the system of beliefs and values that would allow the teacher to 'legitimize' values education as part of a higher education in the discipline; not just those subjects that have values as a central concern. To do this, students and teachers require an understanding of higher education's broader purposes because decisions made on the basis of this are significant to all learning experiences.

Six challenges for the values teacher

We found that there were no simple or easy solutions to teaching values, only a long and challenging journey for the teacher. However, teachers can be better prepared for such a journey by taking note of others' experiences and here we summarize the chapter by presenting six key challenges that were faced by those who took part in the study.

1. Teaching explicitly or implicitly

Teaching is value-laden, disciplines are value-laden and higher education is never value-neutral. So there seems to be little point in any of this being hidden or ignored. What is the purpose of what we are doing, what is our concept of an education and how can we teach values? Importantly, how do we know that we have succeeded?

'What's worth knowing?' will be reflected in the conscious and unconscious efforts of the teacher. We teach values indirectly through modelling and through all our interactions with students. We learn about values from the actions of our students and peers. Often these situations raise questions that can help a teacher inculcate specific values that are outside of the dominant cultural frameworks we work in.

The challenge seems to be the decision we make on which way we approach values education. Collier (1993) contrasts a community that relies upon 'absorption' from one that 'lives by its values' with another that relies more upon 'external declaration and enforcement'. None of these are, however, discrete, and even a community that perceives absorption to be more reliable might fail to recognize when the imposition of authority is required for the maintenance of those very same values.

2. Living one's values

A teacher of values might ask 'how do I live my values more fully?' (see McNiff and Whitehead, 2006). To do this, careful reflection on personal values is important in developing a theory of teaching and higher education. How can the teacher be sure that they are living their values? Probably the best option is to open up practice to supervision but this is not usual in university teaching. Teaching is typically a private and autonomous concern that colleagues are seldom invited to critique. If we do invite someone into our classroom or lecture theatre, it is usually for compliance reasons (e.g. to evidence teaching quality as a requirement for tenure or promotion) rather than seeking to provide a space in which to help the teacher reflect on questions of practice and their values (e.g. should all my students have the right to equal educational experiences?). Supervisors can operate as a critical friend whose role in support is to actively listen to the teacher, ask challenging questions and consequently create spaces for new thinking.

Yet the study showed there is also a genuine concern about identity related to conceptions of academic practice and what it means to teach in a university. Academics are not trained teachers but subject specialists and may not even see themselves as professional educators. In this context it does not seem unreasonable to say, for example: 'I am a zoologist, here to research and teach zoology, not values'.

3. The separation of morals from values

Another confounding factor is that the terms 'values' and 'morals' are often used interchangeably and sit alongside ideas about citizenship education or the teaching of ethics. In the present study, respondents perceived morals to be based on careful values thinking about what was right and what was wrong, but that values were the overarching concept related to all our ideas, with the world changing when our ideas about it change.

In academia there is a reluctance to teach morals to adults except where the subject requires this and the philosopher John Dewey makes it clear that we should not go down that route in education (1916). However, the partitioning of morals from values is not that simple. By the time students leave high school, we would expect them to have an understanding of foundational concepts such as 'honesty' and 'truth' but when they arrive at university, they may need to learn about more difficult value-concepts such as 'the right to free expression', which can be seen as a complex question of moral judgement.

> [T]here is something presumptuous about [moral education for students]. I am not suggesting that students are already morally perfect, or perfectly educated. But, if there is any point in treating them as adult, then above all they must be treated as adult in the area of morals. Of course people who teach in higher education institutions may hope to influence their pupils for good rather than harm . . . But this must be done so much on the side and with such self-effacing tact that it is misleading and probably counter-productive to try to analyze and formalize what is hoped and practiced.
> (Warnock, 1975, cited in Collier 1993, p. 289)

Warnock seems to be advocating a particular commitment to a particular form of self-knowledge; a certain level of self-consciousness for the university teacher. How then can we discern the limits of our moral responsibilities?

4. *Indoctrination*

The idea of indoctrination has negative connotations and is a common objection to teaching values, yet academics indoctrinate students into their discipline without hesitation. However, when this is done in the context of values that are seen to sit outside the discipline, then most find themselves on more difficult terrain. Put another way, if indoctrination is about the instruction of a body of doctrine or principles, then we may find this acceptable, but if it is seen in the context of instilling students with a partisan or ideological point of view, we may not. In fact academics deplore indoctrination while recognizing it in their research and teaching and Chomsky (2003) has argued that indoctrination is what universities are about. For example, we impose restraint as we guide students into what we think is suitable for them: read this, don't bother with that; evolution, not creation; journal articles rather than Wikipedia. Teachers can provide freedom and challenge or direction and control, and most adhere to some understanding of academic standards and would expect 'academic values' to be incorporated into a student's thinking and behaviour. These might include, for example, requirements for evidence-based argument or that plagiarism is unacceptable.

Judgements about indoctrination usually stem from an ideological commitment and yet we all make decisions without much evidence because we tend to accept (rather than challenge) the deeper structures of the dominant cultures of the society and the communities we work and live in. However, there are likely to be choices and alternatives for the teacher and it is this freedom to critique or resist indoctrination that is important. Collier (1993) has suggested that indoctrination is only pernicious if it influences individuals to form an attachment to a particular value 'in such a way as to inhibit or prevent debate on its validity' (p. 294). We then have to consider educating students to recognize and resist unwelcome indoctrination.

5. When values collide

The fifth challenge relates to how we live and interact with those who have different values from us. Often it is only when our values are confronted or denied that they come to the foreground of our thinking, and for those who took part in the study, dealing with such moments was a very important part of their experience.

At one level, higher education seems to be replete with value clashes that can seem rather theoretical and that we learn to live with: conflict between strong managerial control and collegial decision making; between teachers who like to lecture and those who prefer small-group teaching; or between coursework assessment and end of term exams. In other contexts, for example during interactions in a staff meeting, values conflicts can seem a lot less theoretical and more personal.

The idea that all values should be respected and that all value positions have some validity engendered cynicism. Our respondents were conscious that different world views divide people and tend to have the effect of closing down discourse. To overcome this, the values teacher may have to cast themselves as foundationalist and produce a set of values or 'ground rules' that can enable dialogue to go ahead. In the study teachers insisted on:

a a climate of trust and mutual confidence amongst institutional members
b basic values of truthfulness, law-abidingness and moral courage marking the day-to-day life of the institution
c providing authority that safeguards minority views from the pressures of conformity, and the orthodox from pressure to innovate
d teachers being open while respecting openness in others.

Our values may also instigate inner conflict in the sense that we become aware that we are not living them as fully as we know we can. For example, we may aspire to a democratic classroom while acting in a dictatorial way. The challenge here is to explore the contradictions in our values and the constraints put on them by ourselves and by our situational contexts.

6. Defending values

Standing up for a value often requires some courage, especially when this is for a personal belief rather than a more abstract principle for which we have less attachment. When such a personal value sits outside of the dominant ideas of a group, there is some level of risk and those who put forward opposing views can find themselves marginalized (Lovell and Hand, 1999). At the same time, the academic will be conscious that to learn, their values need to be open to critique, even though such critique may not be afforded the same respect as other forms of academic discourse. Academia and broader society are deeply conservative and how practice is organized, enacted and judged still tends to be grounded in the 'rigorous' and objective perspective of technical rationality, rather than examining professional knowledge through the lens of values. Standards of judgement based on values do not count as much. Yet values are the foundation of our thoughts and actions and one of the important narrative themes to emerge from our research was how respondents dealt with personal challenges to deeply held beliefs.

Values narrative: 'An old teacher, an old friend'

Dear John,

Apologies that I have not been in touch since Christmas but as you know, we have had such a busy year. What has prompted me to write is an event at work. I am currently helping in an unusual educational research project that's looking at how I teach 'values'. I have not thought much about this concept, while recognizing that values inform everything I do. In truth, I find it quite hard to even express what I understand by values.

The researchers seem to be interested in the sorts of things I do that help my students learn values and when I was interviewed I was asked who had been an influential teacher for me. Of course my father sprang to mind but I also have you to thank in this respect. We got into an interesting discussion about the differences between the two of you. As you know, Dad is a very strong socialist and his whole philosophy of education is about access and how to work with multi-ability groups in a comprehensive system. So there is a strong kind of social justice orientation to his work. Which I guess did inspire me, but I think it was when you were describing foreign worlds, foreign places and adventure, that you captured my imagination. There was an element of getting into other people's stories. Whereas with dad, it was also about the nuts and bolts of running a school, and naughty kids, and trying to get a message across.

When I started teaching in Ontario I was rather reluctant and it was the lecturer in charge of the programme that really made it worthwhile for me. He was so supportive, incredibly knowledgeable and inspiring and he believed in me as a tutor. I even went round to his house for tea and found out that he also wrote about the geography of music, an interest I share. At that time I think I must have reflected a lot on what I enjoyed about different teachers, even if this was not such a conscious act. In my own way I think I have tried to live up to your enthusiasm and your respect for difference – be it a different culture or a different climatic system or whatever. And I also think that your interest in individual students was an important lesson for me. I care as much about what kind of environment I'm creating, and how to engage different types of learners, as I do about content.

When the interview finished, as a feminist, I found myself feeling slightly disconcerted when I realized that I had just told stories about the influence of all these amazing male teachers in my life!

Love to have your thoughts on these matters,

All the best, Martha.

Dear John,

Thanks for your email and questions. Here are some specific ideas. I think that my research and experience with other cultures has influenced how I teach. I am interested in working with people in ways that support their knowledge and also working with them in groups. When I was doing research in Indonesia I was working with agricultural labourers and people who were working in small business. I was encouraging them to think about their needs in the development process and their roles and their relationships with each other – separate groups of men and women. So you're right. I mean in Indonesia particularly, you don't openly criticize other people, particularly in authority. But there was something about the way that my Balinese counterpart and I used visual methods to encourage people to work with pictures, draw things or create maps and tell stories. This strategy seemed to democratize some of the process and people could be critical without it being direct. But it came out and you could tell that they were not only aware of power relations, but capable of analysing these.

When I get students from other cultures at university I tend to say to them that they're being disciplined in a particular academic tradition and we expect certain things. So I am partly encouraging them to play the game, but also saying: look this may not be acceptable in your culture, but this is your chance to say what you really think, if you want to. And most of them jump at the chance.

All the best, Martha.

Dear John,

You ask how I manage safety in my classes? First, I'm very conscious about establishing some ground rules about how we interact with each other. I simply ask the students to reflect on small group discussions that they've enjoyed and those that they've hated and what was the difference? As you might expect, the ground rules that we establish are all so predictable. I could write them in advance of a class! The desires that are most common among students are being able to try out ideas without fear of humiliation or personal criticism and being allowed to finish sentences without being interrupted. Again, respecting each other's differences. Students also want to have fun so there's a need for space for humour, but not at someone else's expense. I want students to be aware of how ideas are expressed in relation to who might be in the group so that people are not offended. In Bali, I was on the outside looking in but in my classroom I am part of the group, having to live the experience.

From what students have told me, most small group learning situations are very agonizing for them. What I find is that they see the whole notion of respect for everyone's views as so 'politically correct', that they are often not willing to challenge each other. How can we have a genuine meeting of minds in such a situation?

I am not the only one to be aware of the disadvantage of ground rules and students have let me know what they think in feedback. Some feel they can't really say what they think because it would be misinterpreted or seen as not quite appropriate. It's almost like I am trying to create a safe space for difference and tolerance of difference, but students feel that it doesn't allow for prejudice. And they suggest that we want a level of tolerance of difference that doesn't allow some to express beliefs they feel very strongly about. These might have racist undertones or sexist undertones or even something around religion. Yet if they don't confront such value positions, then they're probably never going to move on.

When I look back to the agricultural labourers, I recognize that in one way I was being quite subversive and I wonder how ethical it would be to use similar tactics in my tutorials?

All the best, Martha.

Dear John,

You ask for an illustration. Do you remember me telling you about my course on place, power and identity? It uses feminist, post-structuralist and post-colonial engagements with place and identity. I aim to get the students to confront their own senses of themselves in the world. And this is where some of these criticisms have come up in mid-course feedback. Last semester in particular, I had students really struggling with the fact that they were very strong Christians – evangelical or fundamentalist Christians, and here we were reflecting all this tolerance for difference and the constructiveness of knowledge and challenging meta-narratives and they were going: 'but there's no room for my faith. I don't feel like it's safe to talk about my faith, and yet this is a huge part of my identity'. And so we had to negotiate how to incorporate that into the teaching process. Part of what they wanted was for me to talk about my faith, my relationship to my understanding of faith. I think that being asked to expose more of myself is a way of students wanting to democratize things a bit more. Perhaps if they have more knowledge about me, they have more power, therefore they can challenge or engage or question?

All the best, Martha.

Dear John,

Thanks for all your helpful comments. I got the transcript back from my first interview and the one thing that really struck me about myself, which took me by surprise, was the importance of values. Values in the sense of a faith or spirituality that I feel drives me, and that I hadn't necessarily been conscious of this before. And I was just thinking about how to communicate that to you. What I keep coming back to is that on some level I'm striving for some aspect of holism in my teaching, not to try and capture everything, but teach in a way that acknowledges all the different ways that we learn and understand, that aren't totally tied down to the mind and the rational. So talking about trying to acknowledge an individual or respect an individual, trying to think about ground rules or create a safe space for learning, thinking about participatory activities or getting students to question issues around power, including what's happening in our interaction, are all ways of trying to tap into different ways of knowing, trying to integrate 'mind, body and spirit'.

I went back to the earlier question of why you had been influential to my practice when I felt my father hadn't (or perhaps I have absorbed a lot from my father but I didn't want to be like him!). I know that I said that I was inspired by talk of exotic locations, while Dad is a scientist and a bureaucrat. But more fundamental than that is the fact that you are a practicing Christian and Dad is an agnostic. His faith is in science and rationality but you always seemed driven by some other understanding which seemed willing to accept aspects of the unknown or the unexplainable, the mystery.

And what I love about teaching is inspiring students to wonder, to marvel, to keep questioning but not necessarily to get answers. Dad thinks that you can pin everything down, reduce everything, predict. Knowledge is manageable and will lead to a better society. Whereas I think what I'm trying to do all the time is open up possibilities, which means there will be lots of unknowable aspects which gets into the realm of the spiritual or something beyond the individual and the knowable. This is in some ways related to my research interests because fundamentally I'm interested in how people think they come to know, and how that then influences how they act.

All the best, Martha.

Dear John,

I agree with you and think that being involved in the values research project has given me new confidence and I have been rethinking my teaching this year. The biggest impact has been to allow more space for conflict in my classes. I'm just reflecting back on a new course that I've spent the last six weeks teaching. I know that I don't move towards resolution as quickly as I used to. So philosophically I might have always wanted to open up space for difference, but there was always a concern about how to manage it. And again taking the responsibility for managing it, rather than trusting that it would be managed collectively. I think I'm getting more comfortable with allowing discomfort and disquiet. The biggest dilemma I faced was the value of wanting to keep opening up spaces for student enquiry. At the same time feeling that the students wanted me to put some boundaries around some of those spaces for them. And so at the end of our discussion sessions I found that I had partly stepped into that position, but also I knew that they wanted me to make some sense of the different ideas. To bring some closure or to highlight certain tensions for them. And I don't feel totally comfortable with that and I wonder whether or not much of education is about asking questions we really know the answer to?

Then one of the more able students emailed me after the course (I have attached this, with her permission) and said that the more she thought about the topic and the more that she read, the less she felt she knew. On first reading I thought: fantastic! But, where does this tie in with my ideas around commitment or empowerment? Students may end up feeling disempowered or overwhelmed by not having any building blocks or stepping stones, because everything is unstable, everything is open to question. It's quite a fine line to walk. I responded to her by saying: this is exactly my experience of moving through my PhD – I thought I was an expert on a particular topic until I realized how much I didn't know. And that the more I got into my research, the more I didn't understand. And then I said to her: it's surprising more academics aren't humble as a result of this process.

But recently, I was also challenged by a student in a graduate class. I was trying to be explicit about negotiating my position and power relations and trying to be more explicit about my pedagogy. I referred to myself as British and suggested that this background had obviously informed my world-view. The student asked how I could claim to be working with post-colonial perspectives when I used the category 'British', rather than 'English'? Which hadn't even occurred to me because there's always this conflation between English and British. And I thought: 'He's right.' And that made me look again at how I think and talk about where I come from, philosophically, epistemologically and geographically.

All the best, Martha.

Dear John,

Thanks for sharing those thoughts. I sensed you had difficulty teaching moral values, but in the university context, I believe that it would be the students who would probably have trouble with the term 'morals'. I think my students understand that we are privileging a particular set of values, because the field of gender and development has arisen out of a critique of mainstream Western development, which embodies other values. So at a very simplistic level there's an understanding that what has been regarded as mainstream is bad and what we're trying to do is look at alternatives to find better ways, In other words 'more valuable' ways of doing development. So I think that what I'm trying to do in my teaching is to encourage students to experience different ways of being, some of which I believe are better, otherwise I wouldn't be doing this.

So with my Christian students in the other class, the ideas I raised confronted their faith, but ultimately resulted in productive dialogue and discussion. So much so that a number have come back to me to say that they still think about what we talked about in the course. And in some cases it has strengthened their own faith, and in other cases it has provoked further questions. But they seem quite positive.

On reflection, I think they valued the space to just raise certain issues. They were confronted by ideas around feminism and post-modernism and post-colonialism, but because they were being confronted by those kinds of ideas and because of the way that I'd structured the course, there was opportunity for them to say: 'but what about my faith?' They start to question the appropriateness of particular values being imposed on another group. Which also means there's potentially more space for them to think about what's happening in the classroom, around whose ideas have been privileged and where their ideas fit, be they spiritual or otherwise.

Lawrence Stenhouse certainly seems a fascinating writer and I promise to look up some of his work.

All the best, Martha.

Dear John,

Of course I do hold myself accountable but in any genuine enquiry or discussion that challenges beliefs, there will be experiences and learning that I can't control. I think that there must also be some form of accountability from the student towards others.

I did the second interview a few weeks ago and have just seen the transcript. I was asked if I thought the way I taught was common within higher education and I have cut and pasted my exact response, which I think you might find interesting in terms of your comments on spirituality:

> 'It's hard to say because prior to being questioned I'm not sure that I was necessarily conscious of what I was doing. I would be inclined to say, probably not. Because from what I've heard from colleagues particularly in commerce or management and even in areas of science, the emphasis is on communicating information and facts and knowledge, so that students know things. Rather than say that I have the knowledge and I give it to you, and you take it from me, I'm trying to provoke or prod so that part of my knowledge meets part of your knowledge and something else happens in between, which isn't necessarily directed by either of us and that's where the mystery comes back in, something else happens'.

And then the interviewer asked me if I set an exam for this! I thought for one moment that he might have been kidding but it's a serious question. In some respects any form of assessment seeks to reduce knowledge and understanding because you're having to contain and communicate what might be incredibly complex or muddled thoughts into a form that can be ticked off or identified by someone else as important.

But I have a clear sense that I am on the right track. I was thrilled when the students in my new course this year gave me a leaving card and present, and what they chose to write in that card was delightful. Most comments were about being inspired and stimulated and being encouraged to keep questioning the hard stuff!

All the best, Martha.

Chapter 4
Valuing higher education

New values for old

The university is being reformed and in this process new values are emerging and finding acceptance in the academy. These changes continually challenge the way the university understands itself and the repeated cry of 'new values for old' could be the slogan that both legitimizes and tempts us to accept that our culture is in flux. We now expect change, progress and innovation but whenever a new value finds a place on campus, older ones may become marginalized.

> The exploration of our values and the attempt to live them more fully in our teaching is not, however, just a matter of personal or inward looking enquiry. They are influenced by the social, cultural and political circumstances in which we teach.
>
> (Stephen Rowland, 2000, p. 107)

For example, mass higher education has arrived and personal tuition is on the decline; profitable subjects are secure, those that can't make money often disappear. And this value-contest is repeated daily as the university tries to work out the purposes of its work and how this sits within the wider context of higher education and society. Both 'change' and 'values lost' have costs and benefits, so how might we decide on higher education's values?

A starting point is teachers achieving some clarity in thinking about practice and how the changing conditions in which they teach impact on this. Of course the purposes of a higher education are broad and complex and there are many different, and sometimes competing, conceptions of what this should be. Some purposes are determined for an academic but in modern universities, there is still room for a measure of academic freedom and personal choice in what to research and teach and how to go about these activities, despite the evidence that such freedoms are gradually being eroded by the state and the market (Marginson and Consodine, 2000). At present there appears to be no consensus among higher education's stakeholders on the knowledge, skills and values (in their fullest sense) that a student should have when they leave university and it seems that this responsibility is largely left to the efforts of the individual academic.

Here is an account of valuing higher education, framed in two sections that engage with the ideas of changing purposes and shifting values.

A variety of purposes

Universities tend to declare their values in their mission statements, and other documents that set out what the university stands for (see Chapter 2). Could there be a universal set of core values that higher education might feel comfortable with? If we take the following as an illustration:

- academic freedom
- intellectual honesty
- respect for diversity
- critical thinking.

At one level these ideas might seem reasonable as part of a foundation for the academic profession but closer inspection will inevitably reveal that each will have diverse meanings in different contexts and therefore there is potential for wide interpretation leading to different uses and outcomes. A list such as this lacks a clear referent and purpose, and values need to be understood with respect to the circumstances in which they are realized. For example, Burton Clark points out that 'academic freedom' in the context of a diverse American higher education sector can mean:

> the right to do as one pleases in pursuing ideas; in another, not to have an administrator dictate the teaching syllabus one uses; in another, the right to teach evolution in a college where the local board of trustees is dominated by creationists; in yet another, the right to join an extremist political group.
> (1997, p. 35)

Alternatively, academic freedom is often defined as the freedom for academics to speak their own minds but, as Nixon *et al.* (2001) suggest, this action could be for professional self-interest or for a broader purpose in society. Of course intellectual honesty, respect for diversity and critical thinking all share the same problem of meaning.

So although the particular values of mission statements and teaching plans may be read as worthwhile and may even genuinely reflect an agreed suite of core academic values, they require careful critique and, perhaps as a starting point, to be understood in relation to alternatives. For example, the University of Otago has chosen 'intellectual independence and academic freedom' and it might be difficult for any academic to suggest that there was an alternative to this that would realistically reflect something more important to academic practice. However, there will be contenders to such foundational values, although these are likely to be seen by the academic community as less defensible or even controversial. These include other substantive values that are not always explicitly stated in guiding documents, such a caring, truth, trust, compassion and the idea of conscience.

The problem, as we see it, is that those who work in universities do have a tacit understanding of foundational academic values but these are seldom openly discussed. Our research demonstrated the need for values conversations in which the individual and groups can work out what values are important and what they could mean for practice. For example, what does intellectual honesty mean for the academic, the students, the institution and wider society?

> If pressed, reasons could be adduced to offer backing for this value framework. There is a rational side even to the university's value position. But, ordinarily, one wouldn't know this precisely because of the university's value paradox: the university rarely stops to try to spell out the reasons that attest to its own values even though the university declares itself on the side of reason.
> (Barnett, 2003, p. 121)

It would be helpful if academics and students sought clarity about their values, which would then enable them to take a reasoned stance when critiquing the statements in charters and plans and government documents that seek to influence higher education. This task is especially important if there is any chance that the documents and policies will be taken seriously as a guide to academic life and change academic practices and thinking. If members of the academy fail to do this, then proper consideration of values will not be included in decision making and we may be left with either superficial policy statements that few will care to read or act upon, or new and uncontested ways of thinking that gradually change the values of academic life.

Shifting (or shifty?) values

One challenge in understanding values is that they tend to shift in subtle ways as they evolve over time as societies and groups change. What was once acceptable gradually becomes unacceptable; what once defined a 'higher' education may no longer be understood in the same way. The driving force for change in the university sector in recent times has been the worldwide neoliberal political and economic revolution of the late 1970s (Olssen and Peters, 2005) and the six mid-career teachers with whom we collaborated were highly conscious of the impact of these reforms on their professional lives.

Neoliberalism is largely about economic liberalization through transferring control of the economy from the state to the private sector. Neoliberal ideology is based on the principle that individuals are naturally competitive and if free to pursue their economic needs they will maximize personal gain, which in turn will make society more competitive, efficient and wealthy. In the reform process, power is shifted to private business and the state adopts a new role of ensuring economic freedom rather than being involved in centrally controlled economic planning. No longer do governments intervene as social and economic agents and their main role has become one of liberating business and the market. Concurrent with free market reform and the reduction of the role of the state has been a decrease in government social spending which has impacted on public institutions such as hospitals, schools and universities. The neoliberal state has tended to privatize what they can and ensure that the public institutions that remain under state control respond to the neoliberal principle of competition in order to make them more efficient and less of a burden on the taxpayer (Kelsey, 1998, Marginson and Considine, 2000).

For the public university sector, particularly in NZ, the UK and Australia, there have been radical reforms over the past 30 years that have included new competitive funding regimes for both teaching and research concurrent with the move from elite to mass higher education. Universities are provided with decreasing state funding and what they receive is targeted more towards economic ends. Student maintenance allowances have been reduced and research income is almost exclusively provided to meet economically determined priorities or contracted from the private sector. More recently, it has been recognized that all knowledge can have economic value and as such, can be traded as a commodity.

In NZ, for example, one can gauge the depth of these reforms and the new ideology by how the government views its public universities. In a speech on tertiary education given in 2005 by Dr Michael Cullen, former Deputy Prime Minister and Minster for Tertiary Education, the Minister advises that a university education should primarily be relevant to economic ends. He maintains that relevance and the quality of learning have an inverse relationship; the more relevant an experience is to 'real world and real time concerns' the less one can practice critical thought and so on. With a seemingly easy acceptance of this tension and a willingness to marginalize certain educational values, Cullen declares his neoliberal roots. In fact, the expression 'tertiary education' seems to be part of a political project to dispense with what he calls the university 'brand' and build a new sector consisting of integrated public and private institutions (Cullen, 2005). However, economic outcomes are not the only test of value in a higher education and at present it is doubtful if any Western democratic government would be successful in rebranding its public universities.

To achieve the ideological goals of neoliberalism, the reform process generates competition between individuals and institutions through new technologies of accountability and careful policy manipulation. The sector is micro-managed by way of quality assurance and audit, and, as a result of this, both institutional autonomy and academic freedoms have been curtailed. In the contemporary university, nearly every aspect of academic work has to be accounted for to satisfy the various stakeholders that include government, business, students and broader society (probably in that order). Such control measures are paradoxical in a reform process that claims to prioritize individual liberty. The academic community no longer seems to have the same stake in its own enterprise and is now seen by many as a producer of human capital and knowledge for an emerging knowledge economy.

The reforms of the 1980s and 90s took hold gradually and academics became neoliberal subjects who found themselves responding to new cultures and practices.

Individualism became the order of the day as staff competed with each other for scarce resources in order to survive or advance their careers. As competitive institutions, public universities have had to rethink their purposes, especially those related to the market. Neoliberal reform may have been imposed but there is also evidence to suggest many individuals and their institutions have embraced this ideology and welcomed the new freedoms and opportunities that have come with change. We now have a radically new set of values on campus.

The success of neoliberalism has come about partly because the impacts and long-term consequences of reform have seldom been debated within the broader academy. The dominant message has been that there is no viable alternative and because each small change often seems reasonable, reform promotes a shift to a culture of acceptance rather than critique. It seems reasonable, for example, that with the expansion of knowledge, new applied subjects and professions have found a home in universities, which in turn has led to additional courses and novel research opportunities. It seems reasonable that an expanding sector can no longer be supported by taxpayers, so funding is reduced or reprioritized. Prioritization leads to competition and selective funding exercises and there are always winners and losers. Applied work, the professions and the health sciences have been typical winners, humanities subjects with little economic utility typical losers. Do the winners ever mount a serious defence on behalf of the losers in the new university?

Another strategy that changed values in universities was to make academics more accountable to those who funded higher education (often the 'taxpayer' as a proxy for the state) and then reward the 'correct' type of behaviour or work activity. If we become accountable to others for an activity and rewarded for success, then the nature of the activity, work patterns and values are likely to change, usually to the detriment of other possibilities. If we take the obvious example of research accountability, NZ academics are now held individually responsible for research quality in a Performance-based Research Funding (PBRF) exercise and careers depend on an individual's ranking. This exercise encourages individualistic behaviour, discourages collaboration within one's own institution and provides a new competitive culture within NZ. PBRF and similar mechanisms, such as the UK's Research Assessment Exercise (RAE), have guaranteed that success or failure carries with it both personal and professional cost. Additionally, the new phenomenon of 'being accountable' has a huge hidden economic cost because of the time academics now have to spend on gathering and compiling evidence for the process (O'Neil, 2002).

A further problem with accountability is that it seems to have become an industry in itself and state funding agencies and most institutions have created quality offices staffed by a new type of professional. Those who have investments in this industry promote opportunities for new forms of accountability, seemingly with little consideration for the wide impact it has on the sector. Accountability can change the nature of human relationships with 'trust' and 'professionalism' replaced by suspicion and numerical evidence-based accounts of practice.

Academics unthinkingly involve students in compliance and in doing so prepare them for the neoliberal world and perpetuate a society of individuals who are subjugated by others through accountability exercises. An alternative view is that these types of mechanisms (funding and accountability) have been very successful and that neoliberalism simply rewards those who like clear rules, are competitive and who will work hard for themselves without being too concerned about the gradual erosion of autonomy and academic freedom (Davies *et al.*, 2006).

One may wonder if the impacts of neoliberalism were carefully thought through and planned or if these were just too complex to forecast. If they were predicted, then reform of the universities could be viewed as deceitful because successive governments have gradually eroded particular sector values. Even if the impacts could not have been anticipated, then solving the problems that have arisen with each new reform initiative should have provided the universities with opportunities for critique and contestation. If these opportunities were available, one might question how well they were used.

The new ideology has infiltrated universities to the point where managing staff often relies on mechanisms that would not have been successful 30 years ago. We may cling to the ideal of collegiality but new values compete. One way of starting to make sense of this changing culture is by categorizing an institution in relation to its leading values structure.

In this model, the collegiate university has loose policy frameworks which support academic freedom. Standards and quality are maintained through international communities, the judgement of peers and personal responsibility. The bureaucratic university is characterized by strong top-down management, with senior managers yielding most power. The enterprise university emphasizes such ideals as professional expertise, students as clients and market-driven policies. Finally, the corporate university sees students as customers and values central policy development.

Although institutions will inevitably show all four characteristics, the dominant ethos will be important to what becomes valued in academic work. The public universities have all been forced to develop as bureaucratic institutions as they are called to account for their work and they also need to be business savvy as they respond to reduced funding while striving to expand their operations within worldwide communities. They need to show enterprise as they patent their knowledge or invent and sell new commercial products in the global economic markets. However, they also need a degree of collegiality because the knowledge project is essentially a social undertaking determined by the quality of an individual's contribution to

Table 4.1

Collegiate	Bureaucratic
Enterprise	Corporate

After McNay (1995)

their research communities. In addition, one might argue that a university that leans further towards collegiality is more likely to foster traditional liberal educational values simply because of the freedom that academics possess to make choices about their work, and because it is in this very type of institution that the liberal ideal of teaching and research originated. For such practices to thrive across an institution that has little collegiality there would have to be strong leadership and governance directed at carving out a particular identity. However, even with such a direction, one might question, for example, how a well-functioning bureaucratic university would compare with the collegial university in terms of the quality of its work. To make more sense of the university and its values, higher education's purposes need to be clearly rationalized, yet some ideas are simply taken for granted. For example, who questions securing private funding for new research or the opening up of a market opportunity that will bring income into the institution? Such values may be part of a new foundation.

From time to time, values opposing neoliberalism may get a hearing but in today's mass higher education systems it seems that they compete on an uneven playing field where economic decisions will win out over educational principles. Barnett describes the university campus as a place of values conflict and values trade-offs:

> Caught in the swirls of these rival frameworks, individuals will be making their calculations as between rival epistemologies and ontologies. Practice/theory; engagement/isolation; individualism/collectivity; institution/discipline; and discipline/client; the dilemmas of thought and action are compounded. Value conflicts proliferate, even if unstated; and in the 'one' individual.
>
> (2003, p. 127)

Such conflicting positions could describe the university at any time in its history and reminds us that the academy has never been value-free or free of competing ideologies. However, there was a time when the exchange of ideas and knowledge in broad academic communities was much easier while in contrast, the rise of neoliberal reform introduces new values of bureaucracy, enterprise and intellectual property that do not rival, but replace, other ontological and epistemological arrangements.

Set against this story of competing values and marginalization, it has to be questioned how well the traditional liberal educational view has managed to survive into the twenty-first century. Learning as its own end has largely been supplanted by learning as a means to an end, with the ends now related to the knowledge economy. Teaching and learning are in the economic spotlight and this has impacted on students and their experiences. Students have been socialized as fee-paying customers but user-pays arrangements require that the user has some understanding of the economic relationship between their investment and what they will receive for their money in the short and long term. It is doubtful, however, that most students have the experience to judge what is genuinely beneficial for their learning or even what a quality education is. Yet the credential handed out at the end of university study has become a form of currency of much greater importance as students compete with many more of their peers who have also experienced education in the new mass system. University seems to be a right of passage for those wishing to maximize economic gain and, for those seeking an education for work, the boundary between institutional learning and working life that was previously crossed at the conclusion of high school is now traversed with the award of an undergraduate degree, soon to be supplanted by a masters or even a PhD.

Values around knowledge have also shifted with the 'knowledge explosion'. New fields have generally come from scientific and technological advancement with the resultant fragmentation of knowledge areas and new specializations. These find their way into the university and some new fields seek to claim the status of the older established disciplines, perhaps asking to be judged on alternative criteria such as the ability to generate income. An academic can research and teach almost any subject (which would seem to be educationally liberal), however, what is 'current' is likely to have emerged through a long chain of market-driven considerations. Does the new field attract external research funding? Does it align with the government's education strategy? Will the subject appeal to enough students to make a course viable? What arguments are necessary to convince others that this knowledge area has a rightful place in an institution of higher learning? There is no doubt that market concerns now have a powerful influence on who and what finds a home in our institutions.

Yet it could be argued that because of this, higher education has become more inclusive and that academics can take advantage of a variety of new opportunities and accept different roles including seeking patents, private consultancy and research with and for industry. Noble (1998) suggests that intellectual activity has become intellectual capital but higher education also has responsibilities for meeting both economic as well as other societal needs. Do we have the balance right?

Values narrative: 'No more than an image'

March 8th

I have just heard the news that Joe has been asked to leave. Made redundant. He taught me in my first year and he's an extremely clever man. Very gentle and self-effacing. I still remember his tutorials very clearly. He never lectured at us and always seemed to be able to point us in directions without being overtly obvious that he was doing it. He had a method of interrogation and questioning, not in a confrontational way, he never belittled. Those tutorials were extremely satisfying and he encouraged us particularly to do inter-disciplinary projects. Yet perhaps the real irony is that they've made him redundant because his courses don't return a profit and they needed to cut some staff. They say that what he taught was too demanding to attract large numbers of students. It's one of the most unforgivable things that the university has done. One of the brightest minds this university has ever had has been trashed. And it just makes me sick to be honest.

When I returned to university to do my liberal arts degree, I knew I wanted to be an academic. Yet I discovered that since leaving high school I'd forgotten how to think. How to read a book of non-fiction, to think about it, to interrogate it and debate it, my mind felt rusty and creaky and I had to get it geared up again. But once I got going I never wanted to lose that sense of excitement and inquiry. I wasn't sure what teaching was going to be about but I knew that I wanted to be a good teacher. I wanted to share with my students the exciting things that I had discovered.

Like Joe, I try and offer good and challenging courses, but I'm a lot more concerned with the bells and whistles than I should be and sometimes I'm not sure that the content is as rigorous as it could be either. I get more pleasure and satisfaction out of my graduate teaching and my honours' class than undergraduate teaching. At undergraduate level we've got big lecture classes and tutorials with up to 18 students in them, and massive marking loads, that are steadily increasing. The whole environment is such that it's not possible to be the sort of teacher I would really like to be. There are a lot of stopgap measures and I sometimes feel that I just go from class-to-class and assignment-to-assignment and hope that I'll do my best and not slip up anywhere.

March 9th

I've got 40 per cent American students this year. Exactly why that is I'm not clear. And in the past, they have been my most vocal and enthusiastic students in a tutorial. I have one tutorial that's got eight Americans out of 14 students yet half of them won't open their mouths. They sit there like frightened rabbits. They look entirely bewildered by what's going on and I think that they don't want to open their mouths in case they get accused of being war-mongers. And I must admit that I have had to temper my comments about the current situation on the war in Iraq, which I feel very strongly about. I haven't refused to discuss it but I have decided not to use my teaching as a platform to expound at length on my views because I think that on one level it could contribute to a sense of this being an unsafe environment that could impede learning and leave people, that to me seem already a bit vulnerable, quite threatened. And I'm not sure how to temper that because my opposition to this war is deeply felt, but my concern for my student wellbeing is also something that I feel very deeply about and it becomes a case of trying to temper the two.

March 12th

There's a tremendous amount of disquiet about Joe and the more I hear the more I am convinced that a grave injustice has been perpetrated. Its under litigation at the moment, he's been supported from the highest levels of the universities and a number of professors have spoken up on his behalf. A bright mind who doesn't cut it in the environment where the university is a provider and our students are consumers. And I think it's tremendously sad.

I guess it throws all of our practices into doubt doesn't it? I mean what do I do when I teach a course? I try to make it exciting and interesting and keep the student numbers up and give them a bit of entertainment and I would say there's a bigger entertainment factor now than there used to be. I use PowerPoint, I use video, I use slides and I have authors come in and read to students and they can question them. And none of this is actually necessary for me to teach what I want to teach. But all necessary for students to say: this is a great course and this guy does a great job. And you know: he's worth the money you pay him. If I sit down and make a straight-out effort to engage with them intellectually, how many of them would still want to come to my courses?

I ask myself why I haven't spoken up more loudly about the treatment that Joe is receiving? I guess it's because I provide the sole income for my family at the moment, and with small children I'm frightened to put my neck on the block. So I have done certain things for him, privately, but I guess I'm one of many who has looked at the managerial culture in this university and decided that grudges can be held for a long time and you're better to keep your mouth shut. There are, fortunately, enough senior professors who are prepared to go out and bat on Joe's behalf. It's not a great threat to their careers and livelihoods and they're not particularly worried. But as a colleague and friend I don't think I've been as out there for him as I should have been, or would have been, if I had no dependents.

Joe didn't parade his intelligence and I think of him as a 'participant in the enterprise of learning'. He was friendly. He took time to socialize. We were a first-year tutorial class and he took us all down to the pub at the end of the course and we all sat round for an afternoon and chatted about sociology and philosophical theory and things like that. I kept in touch with him and when I got my PhD scholarship he said to me: value this moment, its going to be one of the few times in your life you're going to get to sit and have time to really think. And he was perfectly right. Since I got my job, the times I've had to actually sit and think about my research have been few and far between, everything is done in a rush. Joe was someone who – it almost sounds corny – but he loved the life of the mind. And he was an inspiration in that respect.

He valued learning and knowledge for its sake. Not for any other reason than he loved to think and have new ideas and it wasn't to advance his career, and it wasn't to show that he was better than anyone else, it was because it excited him – it clearly excited him, and that excited me. Obviously he's not the sort of teacher that appeals to everybody. He expected a lot from the students, but when you rose to his level you got a tremendous sense of achievement. And there was a sense of quiet achievement in himself as well, when he knew you could do it. But you had to realize that you could do it yourself.

It's just as clear that people in the university don't value what Joe has to offer to the extent that they are happy to use all sorts of means to get rid of him. They want a scapegoat, and he is it. Someone has to go and he is going to be the least costly. Maybe I am a bit naïve, because I believe in the idea of the college, of a fellowship of scholars and learning. That a university is a place where this should be valued and protected rather than weeded out and discarded because it doesn't fit into some fiscal model of how a modern institution should function.

March 14th

My American students are still quiet as mice and this clearly has a lot to do with the war. I have been trying to get them to relax and open up but at the same time, I have very strong feelings about the conflict. Just the sheer illegality of it. So I have been juggling with my own conflict and although I have skirted the issue entirely, I need to bring it out into the open and talk about it. Especially because there are always contentious issues to deal with, many of which are closely held by students. I think the first thing I have to do is get dialogue and debate going. Some will sit quietly because they don't want to offend anybody, yet someone will be prepared to jump in. I guess what bothers me most of all is judgements will be made without information and I think the most important thing I can do is show people how to obtain information, not tell them what I know or what I think I know, but equip them with the necessary research tools to find it out for themselves. And that's one of the things that I think I've always worked towards at every level. Equipping people with the means to find things out. I don't want my personal politics or my inner deep sense that there is something really quite obscene about the war, to come in to my classroom. I will talk about the ways of finding out things. But I must admit I have already pointed them towards a website which collects narratives about how the war is being reported and about the sort of things that are being said and aren't being said.

I think I learned a lot from observing Joe. I also think my teaching came about from growing up in an evangelical church which gave me the chance to do a bit of public speaking, you were expected to stand up and say things, so I don't fear talking to an audience. And I don't have a problem with lecturing where there's a huge performance element involved. If a teacher stands up in front of 200 people for 50 minutes, the only way to keep them involved and interacting with your ideas is to entertain them to a degree. How I choose to do this is debatable. With tutoring I have a few basic rules which are to try and engage with students on a one-to-one basis, to get them to participate, to encourage them to think and for me to be very honest about what I know and what I don't know. No fudging it.

March 18th

Very angry and disappointed with my students today.

March 19th

Just couldn't write yesterday. I had a number of students go and complain about me to the Student Union. That for me is probably one of the hardest teaching blows I've had since I started this career. I've always prided myself on being a good teacher, I have good teacher evaluations, and my courses always get the high ratings of approval from students, and numbers in my courses steadily rise!

March 20th

In some ways it's been quite traumatic this year. I am teaching a full year's course in three months and Lyn has been quite sick before and after the baby. I've been trying to do all this teaching and be there for the family and things slipped. And I didn't get the website hosted that I had stupidly promised. I explained to the class that this was my situation and that I intended to make up for it in lectures and course hand-outs. So it's very demoralizing to be complained about. Very hard on my ego and I admit, has left me with a real sense of resentment to that class and a feeling of not wanting to go that extra mile for them. Especially at 2 a.m. this morning as I was sitting there trying to get notes together for this missing website for today's lecture.

April 6th

When I look back to the entry of March 19th, I realize how upset I was. I think it came down to probably two or three people out of 150. The class has now been evaluated and I got extremely good comments, a very high level of satisfaction for the course. I think there are people who, for whatever reason, decide they don't like you, maybe you said something they didn't like or you didn't let them have an extension for an essay and that goes with the territory. Yet to be complained about and sort of summoned before the student president was a little bit hard to handle at that stage. I was under a tremendous amount of stress. I always put a lot of work into teaching and to be unfairly criticized like that was a bit hard to take, when I felt I'd taken every step I could to redress the situation.

Students are very involved in their own lives, they have no conception really that their teachers have lives of their own that can be demanding at times and when you know that you're giving more than really you're physically or mentally capable of giving. Then to have members of a class turn round and, despite explanations, go behind your back and make complaints. I'm not saying the complaints weren't necessarily justified, but they were extremely disappointing. It has left me with a bit of a jaundiced view of some of my classes and at first it was an effort to want to actually really engage with them. But I am starting to enjoy my classes again and getting some satisfaction out of the teaching. Yet something reciprocal does not seem to be there. Maybe it's not intended to be a reciprocal thing, maybe that's idealistic.

April 7th

I don't like telling students what to think, I don't think that's my place. I want them to learn how to think. Although they are interested in what and how I think, I wonder if I let them know often enough? Do they feel cheated? I often couch my thoughts in a joke or a throw-away comment in an attempt to remain neutral. But the American students knew that I was against the Gulf War. That joke I cracked about the US administration certainly gave out signals, but not intentionally. I guess that the way we think structures what we do. Although my opinions are quite strongly held, I have this problem about inflicting them on people. Which comes right back again to my upbringing and the church. I don't want to just stand up and say: this is right and this is wrong. I rejected that long ago.

April 21st

Work over the last couple of months has been so demanding and demoralizing in many respects. So far I have managed to stay out of university politics but now feel enmeshed. I'm annoyed with myself that I've got involved and I need to get back to first principles. There are certain things that I don't want to have anything to do with. Stick to the things that matter and that I'm good at.

I teach literature. I am not the students' parent or the jolly big brother that gives them the keys of the doorway to adulthood and intellectual freedom. I don't want to be the authoritarian figure telling them what they should think. Although I believe that this has happened a little bit more lately. I have been structuring teaching to achieve certain ends and these have a very large values component attached to them. And that goes all through my courses.

I am interested in how people with different ways of negotiating their position within a culture encounter each other. I tend to talk about it with most of my students: how do we define who we are? How much control do we have over the way that we're presented? Or the way we present ourselves? How do we make judgements about other people? And I always say to them in a tutorial at some stage, that the tutorial is a particular cultural nexus and we all have our roles. You're the student and I'm the teacher. Tonight when I go home I stop being a teacher and I become daddy, and there are small people who have demands on me that are entirely different to your expectations of me, but all of those things and these various groups that I operate in go into making up my cultural identity. What are the groups that you operate in? Which ones are you excluded from? How do these narratives that you're engaging with represent the groups that you operate within or what do they tell you about groups that you have no access to? It's all about defining one's place in society and one's identity, and these are fundamental to my teaching. It has been pointed out, time and again, that teaching isn't considered the most important activity by this university.

May 14th

Getting near the end of teaching and feel that I have not kept this diary as I should have. This semester I have been dealing with issue-by-issue and moment-by-moment. Sometimes I've not been as on top of things as I'd like and the pressure has been too much. I have often found myself in a firefighting situation, which I don't enjoy. It quite often seems to be a mode of work I end up in.

When I think about values, I am teaching them quite directly. What I always ask my students to do is read against the grain. To find out who is speaking and who isn't speaking. Who is the narrator in this novel? What are they telling you? What aren't they telling you? Who in this novel is never given a voice but is only observed through somebody else's eyes? What does it tell you about the relations in that society? Are they hierarchical relations or gender relations? Whose point of view is privileged and who is silenced? And it can relate to all sorts of things: how was this novel received in that time? What happened to the author? Was he or she celebrated for what they did or vilified for it?

I don't think that I say: this is how I think it should be seen. For example, one of the things we do with one of the novels from the 1960s is to give three or four different readings from it from particular theorists. And that serves a number of functions. It gets the students familiar with a range of critical approaches to one text that helps them realize how the critical theorist's mind works. I try to point out to them that whether they believe it or not, they have a theory of reading. They have an idea of what a novel should do. They expect a detective story to have a crime and to solve it at the end, they expect a romance to come to some sort of happy resolution. So they have certain expectations and they may not think it but they're critical theorists because of those expectations. What I then encourage them to do is be aware of their own theories of reading. And to interrogate those and to interrogate the way other people read and to pick a text apart.

I don't think it is possible to be neutral in the classroom. I think it would be betraying myself. I do have certain values and I do have certain beliefs. I think the best I can do as an academic is not to throw my values in other people's faces and say: these are better than yours. But to encourage my students to think about what they believe and to think about what their values and beliefs are premised on? I am not sure what my students understand by values. I would imagine that a lot of them would see them as the list of restrictions placed upon them by parents and elders: you do this and don't do that. And perhaps the things imposed on them by society. They generally rebel against that and maybe confuse values with moral imperatives. I guess because of my upbringing I have a tremendous suspicion of any homogenizing discourse and anyone who says: we're right and everyone else is wrong. And I certainly don't try and shove all my own beliefs down anyone's throat. But I'd challenge anyone who came out with a dogmatic position on something and at least ask them to question it.

I do work to unsettle students and that's where tutorial topics and tutorial readings and examination questions tend to operate – at the level at which the text discomforts. From time to time you'll get some students who are offended by a particular text. A few years back there was a play that a number of students didn't like. We had a very reasoned discussion about it and it turned out to be a very productive experience and in fact one of the students who didn't like the play happens to be one of my best research students at the moment. And out of that came a very valuable discussion. Students have to question. Not take things at face value. That probably alarms me more than anything else – the number of students who either read things from their own very fixed position or take things that they believe at face value and don't try and find out the truth or other versions of that event. And so I guess it's in my nature to encourage students to become sceptical readers. Joe taught me that. Set your rhetoric detectors on high and interrogate a text.

October 1st

Rereading this work has given me an opportunity to think back over the year so far. I realize that I have a personality that likes to be liked. And it really bothered me what students thought about me. To be complained about was a bit of a blow to my ego. It seems to matter less to me now and the majority think that I'm alright. I think the more important thing is that my students are taking something of value to themselves out of my courses and lately I've been gearing them a lot more towards that. So I don't use technology anymore to give them a fun lecture. I'm happier now just to make them work and to get their minds thinking about issues even if that is demanding on them. It is quite a trick to lead a stimulating debate that on one level can lead to considerable discomfort. Balancing intellectual engagement with a level of discomfort that students in a tutorial can tolerate. But that's something that my area of literary study allows me to do.

A long time ago I was able to work out what didn't work for me about the church, but I still have not sorted out my feelings about the institution I now work in. I do think the university is important for creating space for people to think. Yet its very rare that people are given the time to sit down and really think, to talk, to argue and debate, and hopefully to work for some general betterment of the human condition. But I like to think it's possible.

Chapter 5

Foundational values

In spite of radical change, there are foundational values around knowledge and academic practices that have resisted change and have protected the university as a distinctive organization. Here we examine two foundational ideas that reflect concerns expressed by our respondents. The first is about the public nature of academic work and the second looks at how reforms have either been accepted or resisted when values are challenged.

The public academic

Universities are part of the society to which they belong and cannot be understood as being separate from it. However, they can also be perceived as being distant because the way in which they serve society is not always obvious to those outside. The primary functions of knowledge construction and dissemination, providing a repository of knowledge and expertise, and a role as a critic and conscience for society may not always have a direct or clear relationship to society's needs. Various national governments have seen universities as too distant and have felt that older traditional liberal practices can no longer meet their requirements. To counter these shortcomings governments have sought to bring the university into a closer relationship with society to meet pressing economic needs. Reform has been successful in shifting practices towards production but seems to have been less effective in directing other forms of social change or the wider contributions that a university can make.

The grand claim of a liberal education is that it frees educated people to contribute to society and perhaps make the world a better place to live in. In fact, it could be argued that the privilege of a higher education places a special responsibility on students and academics to give something back to the society they serve. In most contemporary descriptions of liberal educational values, there is still a place for the public intellectual and informed participation in community life (Axelrod, 2002).

Values, such as tolerance of diverse ideas or contributing to community life, have a rightful place in all disciplines and the idea of the academic as a public intellectual is seldom seriously contested, although it is often ignored. In the research-led universities in our study, because academics were mainly accountable for research and teaching, service sat on the periphery of practice and was clearly undervalued within the system. However, institutions can stand for certain values even if they don't perform these as services (Beck, 1999; Giroux, 2002) and the idea of value-potential is important in considering the university's role in society. For example, free and open debate appear to be the only way of preserving our modern western liberal democracies (Harris, 2005) and Altbach (2001) suggests that a commitment to academic freedom is a barometer of wider political and social freedoms and a clear link to an open democratic society. Freedom to be critical may be the distinguishing feature of a Western higher education as 'being critical' can serve both the economic and social aims of the university and seems resistant to manipulation, at least in more open societies.

> [W]e find hope that higher education can offer a countervailing force in society, distinct from and, if necessary, in opposition to the dominant voices of the day.
> (Barnett, 2000, p. 54)

Where being critical is valued, academic freedom is protected and the academic can use their knowledge and expertise to speak out on certain issues. This right is guaranteed by the state and broader academic community through systems of public peer review. Such a responsibility and potential also lies with students.

> [H]igher education . . . is one of the few public places left where students can learn the power of questioning authority, recover the ideals of engaged citizenship, reaffirm the importance of the public good and expand their capacities to make a difference.
> (Chomsky, 2003, p. 54)

There is a common charge on academia to provide a role as 'critic and conscience of society' and this is seen as essential for the university to contribute to the democratic project. This charge tends to be part of the higher education sector's ethos but in NZ it is also built into current legislation (Education Amendment Act, 1989, S162). Accepting a role as critic and conscience of society is one of the five key activities that defines a NZ university, however, understanding the role 'critic and conscience' can be problematic. Roberts (2007) suggests that providing a conscience on behalf of society is challenging and he prefers the idea of being an intellectual of 'good conscience' which is achieved through living up to the ideal of the intellectual life. However, because a conscience is an internal voice that reflects our ability to distinguish between right and wrong, it is therefore a basis of our moral values. Developing such values requires the ability to reason and reasoning (or being critical) requires a conscience, if the position is accepted that our beliefs and actions depend on our values (Harland *et al.*, 2010).

The NZ Education Amendment Act therefore does not charge academics to accept two tasks, but a single task, in that we have to be both critic *and* conscience at the same time. Furthermore, if we accept Dewey's (1916) position that educators should not give society lessons in morals, then a critic and conscience role will need to be realized through conduct, perhaps living up to the ideal of the intellectual life, or through empowerment, in which students and those outside of the university environment are encouraged and helped to become critically conscious as they develop and care for their own knowledge and actions. How well academics have satisfied these functions is open to debate.

The liberal educational ideal has so far been lived out in less than ideal conditions. The knowledge project could be said to have been a success (the university can produce knowledge of the highest quality) but there have been historically pernicious circumstances that have given the university a poor legacy. Throughout much of the nineteenth- and twentieth-century universities have marginalized or excluded on the basis of class, race and gender and they have been accused of being closed and insular while operating outside of and to the detriment of the societies that they serve. Many teachers have been isolated from wider societal, economic and political concerns while it is these very same issues that have shaped higher education's practices.

The idea of the public intellectual seems to look very different for each member of the academy and providing a service for society or acting as critic and conscience is at one level epistemological and related to discipline, and at another level, personal, ontological and highly political. For example, the potential to talk about critic and conscience ideas must be different for a lecturer in moral philosophy or a lecturer in food science or a political theorist. They may all have different ideas about, for example, fundamental social transformation. The scientist might seek technological solutions to food shortages, while the political theorist may be concerned about social order and issues around inequality.

Furthermore, in the Western liberal democracies, knowledge is usually seen as conditional and that it must be freely open to critique by all members of society, whereas such a foundational principle seems to be more problematic in cultures that have less open political systems or culturally different views on knowledge. We would suggest that in a serious consideration of values teaching, there needs to be some careful thought about the relationship between what it means to have a higher education, the nature of a discipline and what is permitted in the society in which the academic works and lives. A strength of the Western democracies is that the state allows the universities some freedom to act as its 'intellectual conscience' (Wyatt, 1982).

In the previous chapter we argued that values are shifting and the more the university becomes focused on its economic project, the less time and inclination it will have to provide a public role. Academics will have less freedom because control of their activities will be gradually surrendered to the state, industry and students as customers. Will these new masters emphasize economic advantage rather than the other purposes that higher education presently serves? Academics need a degree of protection from such pressures while keeping in mind that they have a special responsibility to use their freedoms carefully for society as opposed to being self-serving critics who work for their own ends. Society does not need critics without a conscience.

Capitulation and resistance

In 1987 Allan Bloom wrote that only the 'embers' of the liberal ideal exist in the American university and we would suggest that nothing much has changed since. Higher education has not rekindled these embers but, importantly, they have not died out. On the one hand, the sector has capitulated to reform and on the other it has resisted change and stood firm for its core values. All those who took part in the research for this book experienced this tension as they worked with the competing pressures of undesirable change and deeply held beliefs.

Capitulation

After such a long period of reform, the main story of higher education and academic life has become one of adaptation to a changing world with ever increasing demands on time. There seems to be a degree of acceptance in the academy, especially towards some of the technologies of change. For example, the idea of external audit and accountability is not seriously contested even though dissatisfaction is typically expressed, which can lead to modification of the process without ever radically reforming the core compliance activity. Research assessment is an example of this situation and in NZ, the UK and Australia there has been much debate about how assessment can be done but fewer voices disputing whether or not it should be done at all. The positive side to such accountability (e.g. increased research production in economically important areas) also has a negative side (e.g. the loss of non-economic subject areas). Despite many such pros and cons, the principle of research accountability is now an acceptable idea and doing without such a mechanism has not been genuinely considered by those who use the exercise to make judgements about the sector, or from those inside the academy. All forms of compliance have unintended consequences and in the case of academics, whose career may depend on how they are judged, evaluation can be harmful because it drives compliance and risk aversion in the new environment. Being risk averse may result in decreasing standards and in the end it is the academics and students who miss out without even being aware of the lost opportunity. Barnett (2003) calls this phenomenon a 'recipe for disaster' (p. 44).

In reality, we have little empirical evidence to support such ideas about the costs and benefits of any compliance technology but the point is that although complex reform will have both beneficial and detrimental effects, the pattern seems to be that change is grudgingly accepted, refined around the edges and then embedded in practice and thinking. Radical alternatives, for example, removing a mechanism completely, is seldom, if ever, seriously considered and in this sense, the academic community could be charged with capitulation.

Resistance

Another way of framing the changing values of higher education is to be mindful that there are many different conceptions of academic work and its purposes, and that not all academics come to work to generate income or see the university as a site of production. Similarly, not all students will see themselves in a client-customer relationship in the act of purchasing a degree. We argue that there is something fundamental about a higher education that has not been altered by the reform process and that there is a bottom line to academic practice that is resilient and difficult to cross. When we speak of 'resistance' we mean refusal to allow erosion of the foundational values of practice.

Universities show inertia to reform because they are large organizations that change slowly. This inertia is also due to the university's public position and relatively autonomous position, which gives it an authority and status to closely rival that of the state. Universities and governments probably frustrate each other from time to time but both recognize that there are certain conditions that are essential for academic work to be done at this higher level. If these conditions are destabilized too much by reform (or by poor university performance), then society will no longer have any of the benefits of a higher education; economic or otherwise.

In our study we worked with the teacher-as-researcher in the research-intensive university and their practice required circumstances that always included a measure of freedom for the individual or research team and usually an environment that valued postgraduate teaching. The freedom to research individually and collectively carries with it the need for a measure of autonomy. Handing over this autonomy to the state or business, or even allowing these entities to define the epistemological project (usually in economic terms), threatens certain ontological conditions that drive a person to inquiry in a subject they love. This idea was described as the 'life of the mind' by one respondent and we would add that such a concept is important for all areas of research, including applied and commercial work. Developing ontological competence for handling specialized knowledge goes hand in hand with deciding what counts, including choosing the next research question. The value of the research done in universities is still largely decided by the individual working in the broader worldwide academic community and this group judges what is of quality through peer review. Allowing this judgement to fall into the hands of business or the state is risky for the wider knowledge project and for the academic profession. University researchers then become 'knowledge workers' or, worse, 'mental labourers', and there is a risk that the quality of research and education will decline.

More recently, governments and the market have recognized that liberal educational values and liberal forms of knowledge can also have intrinsic worth and economic utility, even if these are recast in terms of 'skills'. Critical thought and action are required to handle knowledge in the new knowledge economies (Barnett, 1997) and graduates are recruited on the basis of their critical capacities.

Liberal educational principles, however, also provide the foundation of the elite universities such as Harvard and Oxford where intellectual freedom is valued and there is a place for the unmeasurable in academic life. These principles continue to be valued widely in higher education and few would argue that they are past their sell-by date. There are also countless examples of teaching in universities that are based on liberal educational values such as the inquiry courses and tutorials examined in Chapter 3. We therefore create liberal spaces and both individuals and groups provide 'pockets of resistance' that can have the effect of halting or slowing the reform agenda. Such activities make a huge contribution to the quality of the educational enterprise and provide support for the liberal idea that education seeks to offer intellectual self-empowerment. However, contemporary higher education also needs to adequately address wider social needs and the challenge is to do this without sacrificing the pursuit of excellence in learning.

Because higher education has largely embraced change, some commentators argue that individual reactions have made little overall difference (Giroux, 2002; Readings, 1996; Strathern, 2002). Any future developments are also likely to be slow when compared to the pace of the early radical reforms because inertia to change will come from those who have both welcomed and prospered with neoliberalism. They may have little interest in further institutional or sector-wide development or in providing support for older sets of values. Perhaps those who experienced academia before the reforms will be prepared to speak out and defend a different position but they will risk being accused that they are harking back to some romantic period in history. However, there is an even bigger danger that academics are not prepared to learn from the past or subject today's higher education values and academic practices to close scrutiny. Virtually all subjects and topics can find a place in our universities but the study and critique of academic practice itself is resisted by academics and may even be politically discouraged (Harland and Staniforth, 2008). Yet if pressed, most would defend the liberal educational ideal. Who would be against concepts such as freedom, justice, responsibility, truth and intellectual empowerment?

It is in these values that we can still find a foundation for higher education even though our data showed that academics were unsure of how they were played out in the radically altered mass-higher education institutions of today. Within the broad context of liberal values, the aim of teaching would be to educate people who can use their experiences to contribute to society. On leaving the university a student would:

- feel confident that they can make a contribution (ability)
- recognize an obligation towards making a difference (responsibility)
- be critically conscious of their values and aware that values are constitutive of any stand for a better world (living one's values).

A reviewer of this book asked us if there would be a values exam to test if students were likely to make a stand for a better world, but values, like many other important dimensions of student learning, are almost sure to remain formally unexamined in most disciplines. To find out how those who graduate from higher education live out their values and the success or otherwise of values teaching will require further research and evaluation. However, we do know that our respondents felt that their practices had changed for the better after the experience of carefully reflecting on their values.

Values narrative: 'Lucy's story'

I'm in the abortion class.

It's happened again, it always does.

How am I ever going to get this right?

I'd set it up so carefully. The space felt safe, we were stepping back, looking at the big picture, keeping our distance from the subject. We'd looked at the views on abortion that are out there, we were talking about why we might want to step away from being involved in people's personal decisions, all those sorts of ideas. I was cruising along nicely, it was all going swimmingly.

And then here it comes, out of nowhere.

Women who have abortions are selfish, they make frivolous decisions.

For a moment, I can't believe it, although of course I've heard it all before. Who was it? Kate. And I'm angry now. Some of these women seem to believe it will never happen to them. They think we all have the power to shape our own destinies. And why shouldn't they? They've been lucky and it hasn't happened to them. They are assertive, strong women and perhaps they wouldn't ever find themselves in that situation, but I'm trying to get them to think outside the square. To realize that these sorts of things can happen to anybody. To see that there are other women for whom life is not so easy.

But Judith's talking now, taking over the teaching. It's lucky she's there to pitch in and deal with it. She doesn't mind identifying as a feminist, she's very explicit about her views and her identity. It gives me time to step back, get my head clear again. I have to remind myself that, by fifth year, students have strong opinions and sometimes they are reflecting views that they haven't really thought long and hard about. It's a chance for me to work out how to deal with the situation, how to pull the class back to that side-on, professional view of the subject. And I can breathe again now. I can keep my thoughts on the safety of the classroom and the learning that my students need to do. But I do wonder sometimes if Judith's personal openness in class influences the students' ideas about what I think. If they challenge me, I'll talk about different groups and the views they might hold, but I'd never identify myself as coming from one of those groups. We'll keep working on it, I know, and it's good that we are there to support each other. But I would never be that explicit about my own feelings. I don't think anybody could tell where I come from.

This reticence about identifying myself and my views is a professional thing, really. It's what the students need to learn too. They will have to be tolerant of, and available to their patients, who will often come from completely different places to them. Right from when I was working clinically, I've been very aware of the impact you can have on people. Now I'm much more comfortable with what I am and what I'm doing, but I am having to think and react in classes to things that I know myself are sometimes very difficult. I've had to deal with them on a personal level and I have to professionally separate myself from what I'm teaching, so that I'm not influencing the experiences of the students in a negative way. I'm probably pro-choice, but when I walk out of the classroom today, nobody will know what position I stand for.

When I think about it, I've always quite liked keeping some emotional distance from my views. We would argue with our father all the time, about everything and anything; sometimes just to bait him, and that usually worked! Growing up, there was lots of debate, discussion, squabbling in our family. I was probably very contrary, so if somebody said something, I would try to argue the opposite just for fun. I can't remember everything we talked about, but I do remember talking about women's liberation issues, things like that.

It was such a Presbyterian background, with that strong work ethic. I think there was also a strong sense of feminism and social justice in our family that came largely from my mother – for instance, our family was probably the only family in the area where the parents had a joint cheque account; it was unheard of then. Actually, for a person who comes from a church background, my father has liberal ideas about things like abortion – life was never black and white, you know. I think my parents taught me to question things, and to say if I didn't think something was right. In a way, it's similar working in this community. There's always open debate, people can express such a wide range of views. I love it. It provides a comfortable framework for me to think through issues and I find it very supportive at the moment. The people I've got around me, my colleagues, are just so supportive.

But how did I get here? It seemed straight-forward at first. Leave school, get into training school, work hard, come out the other end, go into practice. But there were all those dilemmas, terrible experiences really, for someone straight out of school, and no support to speak of. I'll never forget going to the 'bod room' for the first time. The Anatomy dissection room. It was horrific. We walk in, chatting, laughing, a little nervous and there's 60 bodies lined up. Are they naked? Or are they covered? I can't even remember now. But they are all dead. All in various stages of dissection. The Med students have been dissecting them and we go in and actually have to pull them all apart again and work out how things go and then there we are, working with dissected limbs and legs and arms and . . . That first time was the worst. I was okay (coming from a farming background, I was a little tougher) but Sally and Ben were wrecked, they just couldn't cope. And the lecturer said: if you can't cope with this, you may as well leave and not come back. That was it; that was the sum total of our support.

It's like that was the beginning of it all. We weren't taught anything about the context we were working in, the framework, the philosophies behind our training. We were like fish in water, without realising the water was wet. We were working away without realizing the underlying philosophies of healthcare practice or of differing understandings of health, illness, anything like that. We were swimming away blindly.

It was when I was pregnant with Sam that I made the decision: when I leave work to have this baby, I'm not going back. And I didn't. I left clinical practice and followed my nose. I had a few bad experiences myself and thought: this isn't enough, I need to go and do something about this. I kept thinking about all the other people that were going through similar experiences to me and not knowing quite what to do with it.

I came to university then, and did odd papers all over the place. I tried out subjects like Moral Philosophy, Medical History, Epidemiology, Women's Studies; I was starting to get a real political edge to what I was thinking and doing. Health issues were still my primary focus, but there was a sort of political awakening . . . I was starting to see injustices and their origins. That fed on some of my experiences in healthcare and all these interesting ideas started to spiral out. Finally, I went to Bioethics and found I really enjoyed it – I knew this was for me.

It fascinates me, being here. We rebelled against my father's church background so early, and now here I am spending my time talking and thinking about all these moral or ethical issues. And teaching them! What do I teach? What is it that I do?

The base of my work is identifying ethical dilemmas in professional practice for students and identifying responses to ethical dilemmas in clinical practice. But I think my real contribution to their education is to provide a safe place for them to ask questions and debate. Sometimes a group can start off quiet and you have to work to bring them in, then once they realize that it's safe and you've got a sense of humour and you're normal, they will actually start to let rip with some really interesting stories. I make a space for those stories and I demonstrate to the students that I value their stories.

I provide them with strategies, frameworks, thought processes for how to deal with these dilemmas. I also teach them their professional and clinical obligations. I would hate to see any student graduate without having some awareness of their obligations, somewhere to go with these sorts of issues because I, myself, found them clinically difficult. I know what it's like to be abandoned in a way, with no strategies, no frameworks, not even an explicit awareness of the kind of issues that you're going to face.

I'll never forget that man, Bill Simmons. He was 97 years old and he had pneumonia. I was assigned to give him care two or three times a day. It was clear that he didn't want it. And I felt very strongly in my heart that I didn't want to do it because he didn't want it. But the doctor in charge was of that very religious persuasion; he decided that we had to do everything in our power to make this guy live, that was just the way it was going to be. As if he were God. All I can remember thinking was: have we talked about this with Bill? Has anybody talked about it with me? There was nothing. I tried to discuss it with George, and some of the others too, but they were swimming along blindly as well, so there was no place to go, no help, no assistance. In fact, I could see that they thought I was a little strange to go on about this kind of stuff. Some people don't really think about these things and other people do. Well, I did, and I knew it didn't feel right.

Maybe that's why I like teaching in an interactive way, because it makes space for people's deep-seated concerns, and you never know where it's going to go. It keeps me interested in the topic and in the group; if I was standing up giving the same lecture, it might as well be on tape. Also, I can respond to the particular needs of the group at the time, which may be different because of something that has happened in the last week or whatever. People can ask challenging questions, but those are often the questions that a lot of people want answered. You get a question from a student and often the rest of the class pays a lot of attention to that question. You realize that if only others had the bravery to do it, they might all be asking the same question.

That's why it's important to me to remain neutral in the professional classes; I want it to be a safe place for students to bring up ideas. I think that if I was explicit about my position on an issue, I would shut up half the class. And my role is not to shut up the class, but to get them to think about their position, where they come from, why they might hold that particular view, whether there are other views out there, and why might people hold them. Sometimes I am prepared to disclose my views on contentious issues, but I'm aware that you can close down people's talking by revealing too much of yourself, and I'm there to facilitate conversation. In some ways, it's like being a health professional, you're there to help other people, not necessarily tell them what you think. You're helping them to make decisions for themselves.

But people do ask me what I think. If it's a health professional class and I'm letting them discuss something, I might very well know the answer, particularly if there's a bottom line on something and I have a particular stance, but I try to let them get there for themselves. And then if people ask me what I think, I will give them an opinion. Similarly, you can ask your health professional what they recommend and they will probably come up with a plan of action. But they will then qualify it, so I often do too. I will say: well, legislation states this. Or, our obligation to the patient might lead us to a particular course of action. But if they're really pushing me hard, I will tell them what I think.

I suppose the key issues that run through my teaching are individual freedoms and the ability to make your own decisions, almost the principles of Bioethics. Autonomy, beneficence, non-maleficence and justice, these are the core values of Bioethics that underpin all the teaching that I do in different places. At the heart of my values is the desire that there should be a place for health professionals to go with difficult issues.

Of course, tonight it will be chaos! I have three children and here I am going on about autonomy and so on, and then I go home and say: this kitchen needs tidying up! But I do carry the same values with me at home. I can't drop my values when the kids raise issues in the public eye about suicide and so on. I think the issues we deal with on a daily basis are all part of the big issues that I deal with at work. Abortion involves things such as personal rights and physical integrity. I can pass those things on to the children without using the term 'abortion' – we can talk about personal physical integrity and people's ability to say 'yes' or 'no'. Even when we talk about sex or whatever with the kids (maybe they're talking about going to a dance or a social) we end up talking about all these broader ethical issues.

And where do I go, when I need to talk stuff through? After class, I sometimes have a chat with my colleague next door. We tend to talk about any teaching we've done, whether it has gone well. Why has it gone well? Whether it's gone badly. Why do we think it's gone badly? Has it really gone badly or are we just being overly critical of ourselves? How can we make this better next time? I also have a peer group with a GP and a psychotherapist. We meet on a regular basis and talk about issues that we find professionally troubling. It's professional supervision really. I would recommend anybody do that if they're dealing with sensitive professional issues.

In the classroom, too, support is the key issue; in fact, support and education are very tangled up. My role is teaching ethics, but I'm also doing professional development: I'm teaching them a language and I'm creating a space. I'm creating or putting in place strategies for them to be able to go on when I'm no longer here. You know, so that when they're working out there in the world, they can put some structures in place for themselves. They will know the language, they'll know how to cope and they won't need me there. These things are going to be so on-going, it's no use just thinking that the classroom is going to solve it, it's not.

These students will come up against ethical issues every day. I can remember hundreds of examples. There were people who couldn't get access to what they needed because they couldn't afford it or because the government agencies they were dealing with didn't want to know. I saw people being denied access because they were gang members. These things happened every day, they were not one-off – here's the dilemma for the year – these happened every day. I remember a patient dying on me. He died of throat cancer and he had a massive haemorrhage in his throat. His family turned up just as he was dying; the doctor and I were juniors and I don't think either of us could remember whether he had a Do Not Resuscitate order. And, you know, after that the attitude was: well come on, get on with it. So what, a patient died. They do that.

I think that students today probably do come out with some congruent thinking about professional ethics. They come out with some notion of what good clinical practice is, ideas about patient choice, the limitations of clinical practice, some safe places to go, some ways of speaking about things. There will be an element of transmitting values because I'm reflecting what our society expects of health professionals. But there's also room for discussion about how to get there and we often explore an issue from opposing or alternative viewpoints, so that the students can work out for themselves where they stand on a particular issue.

So, instead of tackling head-on an issue that is dear to the heart or particularly difficult to confront, I might go at it from a slightly different angle. For instance, yesterday I taught a brand new group. I got them to critique a case about a doctor who becomes horribly unstuck in a therapeutic relationship, it travels into a sexual relationship with a patient and it gets particularly nasty and horrible at the end. The students reflect back on why it went wrong, and what the warning signs were. We talk about how it might have been dealt with better. Then they break it down into particular issues and critique those issues. I also use their professional guidelines and look at what's expected of them as a health professional. All sorts of things come up: was a male doctor abusing a female patient, did the patient seduce the doctor? All these comments and ideas and thoughts swirl about and I start to spell out what the professional body might expect of them. Often the students are just learning by listening and thinking about their initial reactions, such as: the patient got what she deserved. So then I might ask why we have a professional statement that sexual contact with patients is always abusive. Eventually, we start to talk about vulnerability, trust, professional standards. The students start thinking: oh yeah! You can see it clicking for many people.

But then having learnt all these tools and frameworks, I find that I'm dealing with child rearing in a different way and I'm also dealing with my partner in a slightly different way. I have to be careful sometimes of the language I use, the way I construct an argument and so on. I do try for a clear separation between work and home. I think a lot of academics do, but I have a slight problem here because my whole life is involved with how we should be within society. It can also be tricky if I'm out socializing with friends and I hear a statement that makes the ethics teacher in me cringe: ooh that's a nasty one. Sometimes I just ignore it because the social network is powerful and sometimes I just don't want to deal with it because I'm turned off. Sometimes I want to switch off and become a distant observer, rather than an active participant in that sense. But at other times I just toss another couple of bombs that make people think and I walk away.

In many ways, my identity is located within the school here and probably with other people based in ethics teaching. But I'm not sure that I could articulate what we have in common as a community. It would be tied up with supporting students' learning about ethics and their ability to deal effectively and usefully with people who are accessing their services. Trust and safety might be common values across the discipline. You're not going to be an effective teacher if you don't have trust and safety with students and patients. In a way, our understanding of patient and health professional needs tells us how to go about dealing with students.

You see, I will always have to face these moments when someone talks about the abortion they had two years ago or the time they slit their wrists. Their story will be out there on the floor like a wound and I will have to face a room full of students, stilled, blank, waiting.

Conclusion

The idea of values and valuing is demanding if such concepts are thought of as the key determinant of all the choices we make in our lives. We present a case that values are personally determined while, at the same time, that it is normal to accept a foundation for values, even if these are sometimes experienced as contradictory to our beliefs and world views. We recognize that some values are better than others and that we can generally agree on what these are. In the university context there are foundational ideas although they tend not to be part of our everyday thinking or even well theorized by the individual. Valuing and value judgements, however, underpin our personal theories of teaching and as such inform this important area of academic practice. It is only by understanding values that we can start to work out the purposes of a higher education.

A teacher can learn about their values and about the values that a student might develop during their university experiences. Learning about one's own values needs to start with an ontological perspective to provide a framework for practice. Such ontological perspectives can be found in the values statements made by universities in their mission statements and other documents, and these can provide a starting point for a more complex personal inquiry. However, it is not usual for academics to study their own working practices or the situations they find themselves in.

We teach values by having them and in this sense we are role models for student learning and we pass on values whether or not we intend to. Because of this, it seems better to be as aware as possible of what we want our students to learn and our impact on this. The values teacher understands that any personal inquiry into teaching will include questions about values. If teaching becomes routine, values can slip from the agenda and then the teacher has to look for opportunities to reinsert value-questions into professional life. In this context, curriculum change is always an opportunity for reevaluating one's aims for student learning and work out what's worth teaching. There are also certain teaching methods that seem more appropriate for teaching values and valuing more directly, such as inquiry programmes and the tutorial. In Chapter 3 we produced a model that uses four possible dimensions that includes values in the domains of knowledge, academic practice, attitudes and public service. Such a structure is intended to guide the lecturer into thinking beyond teaching conceived in terms of information and knowledge, and for each domain we have produced some examples of 'high' and 'low' values that we hope might inform debate on the possible aims for a higher education.

Chapter 3 concludes with six challenges for any teacher wishing to incorporate values as a part of their work. These challenges emerged from what our respondents had to say during the research.

1. Teaching explicitly or implicitly. Values can be taught consciously or unconsciously.
2. Living one's values. How a teacher can be more certain they are living their values in practice?
3. Separation of morals from values. Morals may be a specific form of values but values are not necessarily moral.
4. Indoctrination. Should not be seen as negative as this has always been part of a university's task.
5. When values collide. Living one's values is not always easy, especially when others do not share them.
6. Defending values. Values can be difficult to defend because of their subjective nature and the clash with objective ideas and evidence.

In dealing with such challenges, it is important to recognize that teaching is set in a particular cultural context that influences much of our practice. The major changes within the higher education sector have originated from the neoliberal reforms that began in the late 1970s. Higher education has been recast as an instrument for economic prosperity with a strong value for individualism and competition. The public university is being gradually privatized and as such takes on new priorities that are market-driven, often at the expense of other services that it might provide for society. New values create situations of value-tension such as autonomy versus accountability, creativity and innovation versus controlling policies and procedures, and risk-taking versus solidly secure and staid performance (Hinchcliff, 1997). Academics now experience greater accountability and management control with diminishing public funding, less freedom and less collegiality. A university education for many has become a commodity that is bought and sold without much effort in the transaction. It no longer seems to be a struggle for wisdom as the student and teacher wrestle with their rights and responsibilities.

In our study, the public role of the academic was called into question. For example, should we be trying to make 'good citizens' of our students? Should we be concerned about promoting positive social traits? There are common knowledge values and broader principles that receive wide support in an academic community such as free speech, critical thinking and being truthful, and the community might also make a stand on certain ideas such as democracy, oppression or causing harm. Values are therefore at the core of any social practice and we can ask challenging questions about what is a good society and what is of quality in human nature. Academics may not wish to teach morals but they should be concerned about the implications of their personal impact on students, the values of their discipline and the role of the university in public service. Postman and Weingartner present a view on high school education and the rights and responsibilities of students in relation to societal issues. Students should be:

> allowed to think and express themselves freely on any subject, even to the point of speaking out against the idea of a democratic society. To the extent that schools are instruments of such a society, they must develop in the young not only an awareness of this freedom but a will to exercise it, and the intellectual power and perspective to do so effectively. This is necessary so that society may continue to change and modify itself to meet unforeseen threats, problems and opportunities.
>
> (1969, p. 15)

Should university students not also be skilled in valuing, have a critical disposition and be enabled to represent certain positions or speak out on particular issues? Higher education may want to create wise citizens who have the insight to understand what is of value for themselves and others, to discern what is true or what is right. In this sense, the academic and the student will seek to use their knowledge for the best ends and means and this could become an obligation that is part of the culture of higher education. Academics and students may then take their role as critic and conscience of society more seriously. However, regardless of any conscious or deliberate decisions or actions, the teacher will teach valuing and values and the public university will still have a role in preserving certain ideals. The idea of the university is thus important because it has potential as a powerful shaping force in society.

The academic community has been complicit in supporting change as it adapts to each new situation without serious challenge (Barnett, 2003). An individual may attempt resistance but there is little unity left among those who work in universities. In his book *The Closing of the American Mind* (1987), Allan Bloom describes the ruin of liberal education not in terms of our ability to understand what might be happening in our universities, but that the failure lies 'in our capacity to discuss or even recognize it' (p. 346). Such personal inquiries call for dialogue with others although our research showed that conversations about values are uncommon. Academics now tend to espouse their own causes and so colleagues quite easily threaten each other's values (not always intentionally) as the legitimacy of their work is contested. Our respondents experienced many immediate and pressing demands on their time and working out the broader purposes of higher education is typically not high on anyone's agenda.

> A man with his nose perpetually held to the grindstone will take the grindstone for his world; and he will be wrong.
>
> (Grant, 2002, p. 76)

Reluctance to start such an inquiry might also be explained because academics know that seeking clarity on values and purposes complicates many aspects of personal and professional life. Anyone who has experienced discussion around a value-position or question of professional identity will recognize how difficult this can be, and Readings (1996) reminds us that the academic community can be petty and vicious (p. 181). Add to such potential unpleasantness the interminably slow pace of collegial debate and decision making, and it is easy to see why individuals might want to go it alone and simply get on with work they enjoy.

Academics with a strong value for teaching can become isolated in their departments and those in our study seldom spoke of their teaching to others. When they did, they tended to be driven towards more private audiences and the outcomes of such conversations remained firmly within a small group of likeminded individuals. One hears talk of getting a 'critical mass' of academics together to be the 'champions of change' or setting up virtual communities to share best practice across higher education, yet the main impact of change remains firmly in the original local practice situation. However, we believe in the principle of dissemination enough for fresh attempts to be made from time to time even though change emanating from grass roots has a poor track record in terms of being replicated across an organization or sector. At present, we have a situation where it seems acceptable to have radically different educational experiences for individual students as they journey through higher education and no agreement (between teachers, students and society) about the purposes of a higher education. While this situation remains, pockets of strong value-resistance will remain a feature of the university landscape.

Values narrative: 'The goodbye letters'

25 May 1966

Dear Mrs Patterson,

I want to finish my piano lessons with you. I just want you to know that it's not because you're a bad piano teacher, I mean I'm pretty good at my scales now. It's just I cry after class, I don't know why. I wish I knew more about you. Anyway, please don't worry about it and thank you for the classes.

Kind regards,

Miss Emily Burns.

6 December 1978

Dear Jess,

We never really said goodbye properly after exams, did we? I feel I owe you an apology, because after all the work you did to drag me through training with you, all your belief that I could and should make it, I'm taking off, going overseas. It's a bit alarming, but I'm just not ready to face a classroom. Not yet, anyway...I heard that you got the St Matthew's job – that's really good news. I know that you'll be a terrific teacher...I'm not sure when I'll be back, but maybe we'll catch up again some day. Oh, and please keep that book if you're enjoying it; I can hardly take it to Europe and I'd like you to have it.

Love, Emily.

12 November 1985

Dear Jenny,

I want to offer you something a little more personal than my formal resignation letter. It must have come as a shock to you: it certainly shocked me to realize that I was going to leave. I know that this is a good school and that I can work well here, but there is something driving me on, something in my comfort that disconcerts me.

I would like to record my thanks to you for your care of me as a beginning teacher. I'm not sure if you knew this at the time, but it was your personality and manner in my interview that swayed me towards taking this job, rather than going into the diplomatic service, as I had always wanted. Admittedly, I was ready to settle down for a bit, but that open-hearted way you have of encouraging others into their best selves tipped the balance. I knew that this would be a school where I could find my own ways of being in the classroom.

Actually, I find it hard to believe that I've been here five years. These kids are so good, enthusiastic and always ready to learn. I've been able to teach in the ways I want, working with the students in groups, putting the onus back on them. I'm still not sure why I do so much group work. Sometimes I wonder if it is acceptable; it seems to suggest such wilting confidence. However, there must be something more to it.

Partly, I feel uncomfortable standing there and positioning myself as an expert. I don't feel like an expert. But I do believe that in the right environment, students can learn a lot from each other, as well as from me. I want these children to have some sense of what is going on around them and in the wider world, to feel that (individually and collectively) if they really care about something, they can change it.

Anyway, I hope you'll understand that I need to move on now. I know for sure that my next school won't be as gentle as this one has been. I guess in a few months I'll look back and wonder what I was thinking to leave this little country paradise for a tough inner-city job, but I'm very grateful for your understanding and generosity in letting me go.

Best wishes, Emily.

15 March 1991

Dear Marama,

Well, what a roller-coaster it's been! I've just turned 35 and I think it shows! I started my job at the College this week and on my first day, someone asked if I had found it frustrating being out in the field! Not quite sure what she meant – perhaps she thought that teaching practice gets in the way of a good teaching theory? Anyway, when she said that, I had a vivid memory of that fantastic day we took all the kids out to Port Cooper. Popped into my head quick as a wink and I knew I wanted to write and thank you for all the great teaching moments we had together.

Do you remember, when I had just started and all that internal assessment came into the curriculum? We were a bit nervous, because it was quite a sudden change, but we felt released from the shackles of the old exam structure and then we had that crazy meeting when we brainstormed all the projects we could do. It was so creative; I loved being able to think about what would make good local history and being forced to confront what we thought history was actually all about. I think the artefacts study might have been your idea? It was quite startling how much work some of those fifth formers did. They started off just talking to their parents, but that wasn't enough, they were led on all sorts of trails, to grandparents, aunts, uncles, museums, antique shops . . . all this enquiry, constructing a history and learning that history is embedded in the community . . . so much to come from one simple, familiar object found in the home.

Oh, and Port Cooper. Now I don't know what the locals thought, it was possibly a bit of a shock to have 90-odd high school students descend on the town for a day and race about doing all their tasks, counting pubs, visiting the cemetery, sketching houses. But I'll never forget Josie coming up to me, absolutely excited by realizing that history is all around us.

You know, I sometimes wondered what I'd hit when I very first started at Prospect; new teachers are put through such a rigorous initiation process! But in the end, I loved it and it still surprises me that I left instead of moving up into Lily's job. I guess I'm just ready for a new challenge. I'm worried about all the theory I managed not to learn when I went through training, but I do know that I have lots of classroom experience to teach from. Maybe if I get really stuck, I can pile the students into a mini-van and take them out to the Port! But then, it wasn't just the projects that I valued. It was the experience of working together as a teaching team, collaborating I guess, to generate those activities. I hope I'll be able to hold on to some of that.

I hope you have a good year – it seems as though you have some amazing projects up your sleeve (as always). Do pop in and see me next time you're in this neck of the woods.

Emily.

19 July 1995

Dear Miss Barton,

I have been very sad to hear of your illness, and would like to thank you for the example you have set for me and so many others through your life.

You probably won't remember me; you only taught my third form Latin class and I don't think I was one of those students who often comes to her principal's attention. As a student, I was always a little in awe of you, but it is in more recent years that you have truly challenged me. Your commitment to social justice, your engagement in social issues, have forced me to consider my own obligations to the wider community. I'm not sure what this will mean for me, but I can say with certainty that my thinking and teaching of pivotal national events (the Springbok tour, the passing of the homosexual law reform Bill) are forever shaped by your involvement as a protester, critic and advocate for justice.

I hope that this illness will touch you only lightly; you are often in my thoughts.

Warm regards,

Emily Burns.

23 December 1997

Dear Beatrice,

Well, it's my last day here and time for goodbyes. I'm sorry that you can't come to the morning tea, so thought I would just leave this note to say how much I've enjoyed working with you.

I have a strong sense here that my values are well matched; not necessarily that we are all like-minded, but that we share some touchstones of belief, that our philosophies spring from similar places. I remember being a little disconcerted, then learning slowly to relax, when I started work here and found that values which had lurked somewhere at the base of my teaching suddenly came together with those of my colleagues. It was an unexpected shift from personal to institutional integrity, and one with which I have not always been comfortable. More or less, I feel able to be honest with myself, to ask hard questions and choose carefully my ways of living, but I am unused to relying on such processes within an institution. However, having found it, it's hard to leave a place so collegial, so comfortable, so co-operative.

It's funny though, how resistant some of the students are to our ways of teaching: you can see from their faces that they feel like they've been thrust straight back into school. With some students, I have this constant sense of trying to get around or under their resistance, of trying to hook them in. Of trying to show them (not so much in words, but in what we do): you don't know it all, there's a lot more here for you to find out. You could make this a really fine thing. But it's a tension, because to some extent they have to get there by themselves. I love watching the ones who do make the transition to working with one another and with students out in schools, the ones who learn how to represent their knowledge in ways that young people can latch onto. Really, I want to offer these future teachers the idea that they can make a difference. That they can make a difference to the way schools operate, and a difference to children's lives.

Writing about it, I realize how much I'm going to miss the classroom and watching students go right through a year of transformation. At the same time, I'm so excited about getting my teeth into research. You can blame that paper I did for my masters. It was such a revelation for me to start considering all the permutations of the teaching and learning nexus in a tertiary environment. I'd like to stay in many ways, but let's face it, the College is not – not yet – a research institution and I'm at a point where I need to use research to illuminate what I'm doing in my teaching. I'm also looking forward to being back in that radical, egalitarian environment. I have such vibrant memories of studying English and the energy of our seminar discussions.

Oh dear, you must have thought I was hilarious when I arrived, all spiky and unready to be teaching any sort of theory. And even more hilarious now that I'm going off to university, so that I can be a researcher! But really, it's been good here, it's been fun.

Take care, Emily.

6 February 2003

Dear Marama,

How lovely to pick up our off-and-on correspondence again. It's such a rare thing to have someone I can write to from wherever I am, without pausing too much for explanation or self-correction. Thank you for all your news and reflections. I'm so glad to hear about your promotion – it will be a big change for you, but you will shine, I am sure. I hope that I too am about to enter a more 'shiny' phase of life; in many ways I have spent the last few years moving in fairly constricted realms, caring for Kirsten, writing my thesis, concentrating my focus and energy on these precious, difficult, surprisingly life-giving things. But now some ends have come.

For a long time, I have been developing a concept of learning, and I'd like to write to you about it, partly because it seems to flow from many of the conversations we had together, but also (more selfishly) as a way of untangling some rather jumbled thoughts.

Where to start? It seems very important to me to reject the idea of 'expert' and the idea that knowledge is cumulative, a fixed entity to which you just add building blocks. I have a notion of a university (or any educational institution) as a community of learners. If you think of the university as a community of learners (rather than as academics and students, shall we say) and if you frame academic research as learning, then you can argue that what's going on in the university is a whole group of people learning in one another's company. At different levels of sophistication maybe, according to need or purpose, but when you start thinking in that way it begins to break down the hierarchies associated with knowledge, the idea of knowledge being transmitted downwards, which seems to be very much the traditional view of what happens in the university.

Actually, this takes me back to the transition from the College to the University – there was a huge culture shock in that transition which I hadn't anticipated. I was shocked at how hierarchical, patriarchal, hide-bound the University was. It was so smug. The views I brought with me, about teaching and learning, just didn't mesh at all, although they fitted better in the educational development field. I'm not sure why I'm so anti-hierarchical. I think of education as a right and not a privilege. My father grew up on Clydebank in Glasgow and came out into the workforce during the Depression, was unemployed, then worked in the shipyards and later became an electrician. I think that background influences my belief that everybody has a right to be able to learn to the best of their ability, and that part of my role as a teacher is to make that possible.

Another thing that bothers me is the distinction in the higher education field at the moment between 'teacher-centred' and 'student-centred'. Crudely, teacher-centred is seen as bad and student-centred as good. I don't like the dichotomy. Last year, I got very excited about Bill Readings' writing about 'the university in ruins'. He talked about obligation, the notion of teaching as being this two-way relationship with obligation on each side. I'd always, in my mind, called it a 'partnership', but I like the idea of obligation. He also talks about the idea that you go through university and become an independent, self-directed, autonomous learner. He argues that that's not what we should be aiming for, that in fact as an ongoing learner you are dependent on other people. I'm starting to think of it as being tied into a community, where the teaching/learning relationship continues all through your life, but it differs in who is the teacher and who is the learner. And that links back into this 'community of learners' idea, which I want to extend beyond the notion of 'the institution'. And now I've completely lost where I started this whole spiel!

I find the idea of transformation intriguing. The clearest transformation in terms of my learning has been my PhD thesis; I'm really conscious of the way that it has changed and shaped my thinking. It was hard work and coincided with some fairly big upheavals within my life, but I find myself thinking that to a certain extent it has flowed over into a way of living in the world, although that's perhaps less certain. I probably couldn't have said a lot of this several years ago. Not because it wasn't there; I think that beliefs and values don't just suddenly emerge at a certain point – they're subterranean, they're there from very early on.

However, because my thesis was about teaching and learning, it's probably enabled me to name things and see things clearly. While it hasn't given me that sense of expertise, it probably has given me a feeling of a place to stand. A place to stand. Not a place that I would defend at all costs. I have a real problem with the tendency among university academics to adopt a theoretical position and then slate everything outside that. I like hearing what other people have to say, I'm quite curious about other people. I like difference. I think valuing difference is important, but I don't know where that comes from.

I think there's something else that has come out of the writing of the thesis, and this is more difficult to frame; it's more personal. Although I talk a lot about collaboration and interacting with people and that idea of a community of enquiry, sitting alongside that is me as an individual who actually needs lots of space and who quite likes being on her own. So, there's a tension there. It's strange writing a thesis: although you sit on your own with books and a computer, although you're isolated, physically and mentally, there is this strong sense of connection with the people whose writing you're reading, with people who have gone before you, with colleagues that you may talk to, with supervisors, with your research participants. All these people are informing what you're doing, and are sharing in your creation of knowledge. So, I've come out of writing the thesis with a much-strengthened sense of community again. It's like having all these friends, like you see a world and there are all these fine threads connecting people and ideas and interactions.

Embedded in this is the experience of Kirsten being quite unwell and then in the last year of my thesis getting worse and then her death, which marked the end of a long period of my having to concentrate fairly closely on one person, to whom I was very close but then there's an opening up, there's this idea of linking that comes through the thesis and there's almost a new start of linking possibility that comes into the real world. But sitting beside that is a drawing back as well, a protection of self.

Now I'm wondering about the link with a set of values or perhaps spirituality, I'm wondering where those values come from. I think there's a connection again with community. I'm sure your values are embedded in the community in which you grow up. And they're probably also informed, for somebody like me who likes reading and travelling, by a world outside that community which may in fact be quite different from that community. I guess you sift . . .

Please write again and tell me your thoughts. I feel like I am juggling all these balls and everything links to everything else, but I need some help to hold it all together. Or maybe you will tell me just to toss them up and trace their paths through the sky.

Emily.

31 October 2003

A Not-To-Be-Sent Resignation Letter:

I feel a growing disquiet with my work here. I can't stand feeling complicit in this government/university quality agenda: I will never see education as a commodity or an instrument and it goes against all that I believe to sit in judgement on my colleagues. Yet this is quietly implied in much of our work and I'm not sure that I can shake myself free of it.

At the same time, educational development (such a presumptuous idea) will always be marginalized in the university sector and perhaps that's not a bad thing. But it does get frustrating after a time. I'm tired of sitting on committees where my ideas are clearly coming from a completely different standpoint to those of my colleagues. Where we don't even have enough shared language for me to explain my concerns and values. But I have to ask myself whether I have the right to challenge people in the university who see the world differently from me, whether I even have the right to challenge a view of the world which is atomistic, hierarchical, primarily seeing knowledge as something to be transferred. Because over a long period of time, disciplines have built up their own ways of dealing with knowledge, of seeing the world and inducting people into that world and I'm not sure that I can come in boots and all and challenge that.

Likewise, I'm realizing that I expect quite a high level of commitment from people – students and colleagues. I expect to give a lot myself in my teaching, to engage at a high level with the people I'm working with. In return, I expect engagement, commitment from my students and colleagues. In learning, we engage with a discipline or some knowledge, but it's mediated by people, so it becomes an emotional engagement. But the thought that is turning over more and more in my mind is that people will have different ways of getting to similar endpoints and perhaps some will choose to remain outside the circle, looking in. Maybe I'm ready to say that's fine, that's where they are at.

I see myself as an unsettler, someone who unlocks questions in people's minds and sets them rolling out. This is important to me and I think it is a necessary role to play in a place as naturally conservative as this, a place where opinions and values tend to be entrenched as much as broadened. But this role has its costs and it is only true to part of my being. It's tiring and often it's not very creative. So where does this leave me?

A note on the methodology of narrative inquiry

One of the great difficulties faced by a researcher of human experience is how they discover what is happening in the infinitely complex social world they are investigating and how they represent their findings for others. There is a great research divide between this social research world and the world of natural science which goes about its business with an enviable simplicity. Science inquiry relies on hypothesis testing, gathering empirical data through observation and controlled experimentation. It is largely quantitative with results that are repeatable and generalizable. However, super-complex systems – and this includes most cultural and social phenomena – remain stubbornly immune to genuine scientific investigation. The social sciences may still believe in the utility of the scientific method, but there is also much dissatisfaction with such an approach among its practitioners and much effort has been directed towards qualitative alternatives for representing the complexities of human experience.

So when we set about researching experiences of higher education we find that we do not have one method to choose from but several. Making a choice is not straightforward as this depends on the research question, the context and the imagination of the researcher. Furthermore, a method will not mean very much at face value because each one is understood, interpreted, enacted and filtered by the individual researcher or research team. All qualitative methods also end up as a collaboration between the researcher and those researched and the outcomes of this interaction are influenced by the information given during the research process, the knowledge that the researcher already has and new knowledge that is socially constructed in the process. If all this were not complicated enough, one's personal values and ontological perspectives come into play and regardless of the method chosen there is a unique process of selection and interpretation by each researcher. Then one's epistemology guides the choice of method, influences the research question and the way in which data is collected, analysed and presented.

Where does this leave the higher education researcher or the teachers that we are encouraging to become inquirers of their own educational practices? We suggest that the first step is a value decision as the researcher works out the purposes of their research (beyond an interest in 'finding out the meaning of something'). What is the point of doing the research in the first place? Such a question may seem prosaic but it is one that novice researchers find very hard to answer. It is also a question that can be answered on different levels and if we take our own methodological considerations for this book we can put forward the following rationale.

The broad purposes of our research were:

1. To discover new knowledge.
2. To advance educational theory.
3. To help the research team learn.
4. To help our respondents learn.
5. To help academics from all disciplines learn (about teaching values).

The aim of the project was to realize these five purposes in the specific context of 'teaching values and the values of higher education'. The last point also explains who the main audience for the research is and what we hope it will be used for. These purposes are, in fact, a statement of values that have guided all our research decisions. The work was undertaken on behalf of academics from all disciplinary areas and we clearly wanted to make a contribution to repositioning values within higher education. A researcher has a responsibility to say something useful and something that is also educational (one could argue that this is essential when it comes to the outcomes of research *into* education).

Once a researcher has decided on the purposes of their inquiry, audience and specific aims for the project, the next step is to engage with methodology and select an appropriate research method. We hope to illustrate this process by giving a brief overview of the rationale behind our choice of narrative inquiry as one of the methods used in this research project.

A methodological argument for using narratives

The main chapters are based on a traditional emergent inductive qualitative research process (Thomas, 2006). The outcomes reflect our values and knowledge, and our interpretation and our representation of the experiences of our six colleagues. We selected and filtered the data until the final product became a co-construction of our own ideas with those of the respondents and with theoretical ideas from the wider research literature. In this process of inquiry there seems to be no way of avoiding such an intense ontological personalization through the researcher and research team. We included checks for trustworthiness and credibility by sharing our ideas with respondents but even such verification requires some professional judgement on our behalf.

We also analysed the same data from a different methodological perspective. Because we were investigating a rather nebulous subject, we believed that to make sense of their experiences, our respondents would need to tell us stories about their teaching practices and university life to help them understand and explain their values, the values they taught and how they valued higher education. Eisner

(1997) argues that different ways of representing such data lead to the construction of different kinds of understanding.

We reasoned that we could extract the core ideas from all the stories and fragments of information that each respondent shared with us and reproduce these in a new narrative that a reader could more readily connect with. A reader can then make new realities for themselves that might inform their professional practices. Such engagement opens up new possibilities for learning because there will be an infinite number of connections between each reader and the text.

In its simplest form, narrative inquiry is a method of naturalistic inquiry that allows the researcher to collect and analyse data and present this in a narrative style verbally, visually or more commonly in written form. The key arguments for its effectiveness are that we all live storied lives, talk about ourselves through stories and that stories have great potential for illuminating and helping us understand the infinite complexities of human experiences (Connolly and Clandinin, 1990). In this form of research, the researcher tells new stories that have been derived from older accounts of experience. These older accounts are the data that are collected through interviews and other methods and then transformed in some way to provide the research outcome (Polkinghorne, 1995).

Stories are a different route to understanding our world and there is no doubt that narrative inquiry has now achieved qualified acceptance as a research method by some in the broader academic community. However, it is not without its critics and it still remains on the fringes of mainstream educational research. Like all research methods, it has its strengths and limitations and some of these will be addressed below.

Bruner (1996) argues that reading narratives will be neither rational (in terms of determining a truth) nor empirical (in terms of a method for the verification of text) and we would like our stories to be seen as 'unfinished' research, although we are aware that other narrative researchers would not agree with this position. However, we feel that part of the systematic inquiry inherent in any process that calls itself 'research' needs to be done by the reader rather than the researcher, in part because all texts are individually read and interpreted. Our problem might be that it is not usual to ask a reader to complete the analysis. We are not sure if this rather unconventional request will suit all academics and many may prefer the more traditional representation of ideas in the complementary main chapters.

Connelly and Clandinin (1990) recognize a dual function in narrative inquiry in that it tends to have a major impact on the research respondent's learning. Bolton suggests that 'Narratives express the values of the narrator; they also develop and create values, as well as a sense of self-purpose, in the telling' (2006, p. 206). We had predicted that the long collaboration with the academics who took part in the study would transform the research process and that participation would provide a situation that facilitated reflection and enhance professional learning for everyone. We certainly viewed the research project as a moral enterprise and worked out many of the ethical choices as we went along and refined our method alongside the teachers we were working with. This process broadened our understanding and awareness of our own values for both research and other dimensions of our professional practice. There is no doubt that our values came in to sharp focus during the study.

We predicted that each of our research approaches would have some impact on the other so we carried out the narrative analysis first and consciously tried to leave out as much of ourselves as possible and bracket out theory, so that the participants felt that they had told their own stories without interference. The stories also needed to have 'narrative realism' and accurately reflect academic life if they were to have any validity at all. What we ended up with is something we call 'semi-fictional', yet all the stories have a sense of truth in that they are meticulously based on the data teachers supplied and are then validated by the teacher as both story teller and editor.

> [T]he analyst creates a meta-story about what happened by telling what the interview narratives signify, editing and reshaping what was told, and turning it into a hybrid story, a 'false document'.
> (Riessman, 1993, p. 13)

There is probably no such thing as a true story and so we must strictly label our narratives as a semi-fictional or perhaps as one of Reissman's 'false-documents', however, we feel that it is important that the reader knows that they are as authentic as we could make them. Often, when reading narrative research accounts from other research areas we have been left wondering about this point – did something really happen? We do recognize that ambiguity regarding provenance and truthfulness could itself provide an opportunity for learning but we prefer to be upfront with the way in which we have presented our research.

The stories are told in such a way as to ensure that the academics or their present universities cannot be identified. We looked for the grand narratives in our data and also considered the literary concepts of drama, tense, voice and genre. We sometimes embellish an idea, add more detail from later inquiries, move accounts around in time and use different narrators. Characterization became important in two stories ('East of Kinshasa' and 'Eddie'), but in the rest the main character is the research respondent. In 'Eddie', all the characters represent different facets of the one respondent.

We deliberately experimented with writing styles and genres that might appeal to a reader, aware that in striving for authenticity we could have ended up with dull accounts that would not meet the criteria of a 'good story'. Bruner (1996) argues that genre could be 'mere afterthoughts that occur to tidy academic minds' but we found that genre emerged during the analysis and seemed to have a very strong relationship to the respondent's thoughts and ideas.

Preservation of ambiguities within the problems that academics faced was important to us and we have not attempted to write a sanitized version or to write expressly for 'teaching purposes', being keen to leave space for ideas to be contested rather than proselytizing. We wanted to capture the academic's struggle and to confront the reader with real-life situations with the assumption that this would provide more fertile ground for an educational process, rather than one of moralizing or easy lessons. The final version should leave the reader with alternatives for interpreting the actions of the teachers (Riessman, 1993) and should invite the reader to reconstruct the narrative in order to make one that is more personally fulfilling.

Narrative also enables the development of empathy with the characters and situations (Bolton, 2006), and this is something that is often lacking in traditional research forms. Empathy helps the reader understand a person and this is essential to stories about a professional's values and how they are enacted, although we realize that it will also be the reader's values that steer such a process. Some may find one aspect of a story a guide to what not to do while another reader may connect in quite a different way. There will be both agreement and disagreement over certain points, which could be a strength, but also a potential weakness if the ideas are construed in a way that the teachers never intended when they first told their stories. Yet this risk is inevitable in all forms of linguistic exchange as an individual comes to terms with and constructs meaning.

The challenge for the qualitative researcher using narrative is to write a story that has utility and Clough (2002) suggests that narrative is useful only to the extent that it opens up to its audiences a deeper view of life in familiar contexts. The process is therefore hermeneutic and authors essentially demand interpretive thinking on the part of the reader. Such a position could be seen as a limitation of this research form, especially if the potential reader is antithetical to interpretive thinking or sees narrative as too unconventional.

What our respondents thought

The final stories were sent to each respondent to be edited, refined or co-authored as they saw fit but only very minor alterations were made. In this sense, all teachers were happy with the outcomes and how they had been represented.

> I can recognize practically everything I said in the narrative. The difference is in the other things that were necessarily omitted, and also the fact that I've never written in diary mode, so it seems strange to have my words presented in such a way. Not a complaint, however, just an observation.

> Thanks for the narrative. It both sounds and doesn't sound like me. But I read it through with enjoyment and have few if any changes . . . It surprised me how specific it was to the moment.

> I still feel a little embarrassed by what I perceive to be relatively un-thought through comments and processes about my values in teaching in the narrative, but respect that this is largely how I phrased them to you in the interviews. I feel I have learnt so much through reading my own words and through being given a chance to think about and express these ideas, that if you were

to do the research again with me tomorrow, I would be far clearer and more articulate about how I practice.

I have very much enjoyed this process and though I don't fully understand how it really works (I'll be very interested to see the book!!), I have benefited from being involved, which is more than could be said for many forms of research. I feel that you have facilitated a precious space for reflection and self-analysis which will inform my teaching practice in future, and that through your 'letter' approach to my narrative, you have begun an internal dialogue which will continue to enrich my work and enjoyment of life.

I have just read the narrative. I must say I am hugely impressed with how you did that. It just rang true for me. Such an interesting technique, it really had me laughing as well.

I haven't suggested much [change]. As you will see it's really just some of the personal family stuff that I'd like a little more obscured. I don't think this will be difficult or time consuming to do. For people who know me I'm still pretty identifiable!

If there are different ways to understand our world and different ways of representing this, then we must include narrative forms simply because there is a likelihood that our values are formed and lived through the narratives we hear, those we tell ourselves and those that we choose to tell others.

> We live in a sea of stories, and like the fish who (according to the proverb) will be the last to discover water, we have our own difficulties grasping what it is like to swim in stories. It is not that we lack competence in creating our narrative accounts of reality – far from it. We are, if anything, too expert. Our problem, rather, is achieving consciousness of what we so easily do automatically, the ancient problem of prise de conscience (becoming aware).
>
> (Bruner, 1996, p. 147)

References

Altbach, P. (2001) 'Academic freedom: international realities and challenges', *Higher Education*, 41: 205–219.
Axelrod, P. (2002) *Values in Conflict: The University, the Marketplace and the Trials of Liberal Education*, Montreal: McGill-Queen's University Press.
Bandura, A. (1977) *Social Learning Theory*, New York: General Learning Press.
Barnett, R. (1990) *The Idea of Higher Education*, Buckingham: The Society for Research into Higher Education and Open University Press.
Barnett, R. (1997) *Higher Education: A Critical Business*, Buckingham: The Society for Research into Higher Education and Open University Press.
Barnett, R. (2000) *Realizing the University in an Age of Supercomplexity*, Buckingham: The Society for Research into Higher Education and Open University Press.
Barnett, R. (2003) *Beyond All Reason: Living with Ideology in the University*, Buckingham: The Society for Research into Higher Education and Open University Press.
Beck, J. (1999) 'Makeover or takeover? The strange death of educational autonomy in neo-liberal England', *British Journal of Sociology of Education*, 20(2): 223–238.
Bloom, A. (1987) *The Closing of The American Mind*, New York: Simon and Schuster.
Bolton, G. (2006) 'Narrative writing: reflective enquiry into professional practice', *Educational Action Research* 14(2): 203–218.
Bruner, J. (1996) *The Culture of Education*, Cambridge, MA: Harvard University Press.
Clark, B. R. (1997) 'Small worlds, different worlds: the uniqueness and troubles of American academic professions', *Daedalus*, 126(4): 21–42.
Clough, P. (2002) *Narratives and Fictions in Educational Research*, Buckingham: Open University Press.
Chomsky, N. (2003) *Chomsky on Democracy and Education*, New York: RoutledgeFalmer.
Collier, G. (1993) 'Learning moral judgment in higher education', *Studies in Higher Education*, 18(3): 287–297.
Cullen, M. (2005) Address to the Association of University Staff Conference, available at: <www.beehive.govt.nz/minister/michael+cullen?page=5&type=speech> (accessed 5 November 2008).
Connelly, F. M. and Clandinin, D. J. (1990) 'Stories of experience and narrative inquiry', *Educational Researcher*, 19(5): 2–14.
Davies, B., Gottsche, M. and Bansel, P. (2006) 'The rise and fall of the neo-liberal university', *European Journal of Education*, 41(2): 305–319.
Dewey, J. (1916) *Democracy and Education*, New York: MacMillan.

References

Education Act Amendent 1989. Part 14 Establishment and disestablishment of tertiary institutions, S162, 4(a)(v) New Zealand Government.

Eisner, E. (1997) 'The promise and perils of alternative forms of representation', *Educational Researcher*, 26(6): 4–10.

Elbaz, F. (1992) 'Hope, attentiveness and caring for difference: the moral voice in teaching', *Teaching and Teacher Education*, 8(5/6): 421–432.

Giroux, H. A. (2002) 'Neoliberalism, corporate culture, and the promise of higher education: the university as a democratic public sphere', *Harvard Educational Review*, 72(4): 425–463.

Grant, R. (2002) 'The end of liberal education'. In D. S. Preston (ed.), *The University in Crisis*, Amsterdam: Rodopi.

Grix, J. (2002) 'Introducing students to the generic terminology of social research', *Politics*, 22(3): 175–186.

Harland, T. and Staniforth, D. (2008) 'A family of strangers: the fragmented nature of academic development', *Teaching in Higher Education*, 13(6): 669–678.

Harland, T., Tidswell, T., Everett, D., Hale, L. and Pickering, N. (2010) 'Neoliberalism and the academic as critic and conscience of society', *Teaching in Higher Education*, 15(1): 85–96.

Harris, S. (2005) 'Rethinking academic identities in neo-liberal times', *Teaching in Higher Education*, 10(4): 421–433.

Hinchcliff, J. (1997) *Values Integrating Education: An Exploration of Learning in New Zealand*, Auckland: Mirilea Press.

Kelsey, J. (1998) 'Privatizing the universities', *Journal of Law and Society*, 25(1): 51–70.

Lovell, A. and Hand, L. (1999) 'Expanding the notion of organizational performance measurement to support joined-up government', *Public Policy and Administration*, 4(2): 17–29.

McNay, I. (1995) 'From collegial academy to the corporate enterprise: the changing cultures of universities'. In T. Schuller (ed.), *The Changing University*, Bristol: Taylor & Francis.

McNiff, J. (1996) *Teaching as Learning: An Action Research Approach*, London: Routledge.

McNiff, J. and Whitehead, J. (2006) *All You Need to Know About Action Research*, London: Sage.

Macfarlane, B. (2004) *Teaching with Integrity: The Ethics of Higher Education Practice*, London: RoutledgeFalmer.

Marginson, S. and Considine, M. (2000) *The Enterprise University. Power, Governance and Reinvention in Australia*, Cambridge: Cambridge University Press.

Morrison, T. (2000) 'How Can Values be Taught in the University?', *Michigan Quarterly Review*, XL(2). Online, available at: <http://hdl.handle.net/2027/spo.act2080.0040.201> (accessed 3 August 2010).

Nixon, J., Marks, A., Rowland, S. and Walker, M. (2001) 'Towards a new academic professionalism: a manifesto of hope', *British Journal of Sociology of Education*, 22(2): 227–244.

Noble, D. F. (1998) 'Digital diploma mills: the automation of higher education', *Science as Culture*, 7(3): 355–368.

Olssen, M. and Peters, M. A. (2005) 'Neoliberalism, higher education and the knowledge economy: from the free market to knowledge capitalism', *Journal of Educational Policy*, 20(3): 313–345.

O'Neill, O. (2002) *A Question of Trust*, Cambridge: Cambridge University Press.
Polanyi, M. (1996) *The Tacit Dimension*, New York: Doubleday.
Polkinghorne, D. E. (1995) 'Narrative configuration in qualitative analysis'. In J. Hatch and R. Wisniewski (eds), *Life History and Narrative*, London: Falmer Press.
Postman, N. and Weingartner, C. (1969) *Teaching as a Subversive Activity*, New York: Dell.
Readings, B. (1996) *The University in Ruins*, Harvard: Harvard University Press.
Riessman, C. K. (1993) *Narrative Analysis: Qualitative Methods Series 30*, London: Sage.
Roberts, P. (2007) 'Intellectuals, tertiary education and questions of difference', *Education Theory and Philosophy*, 39(5): 480–493.
Rogers, C. R. and Freiberg, H. J. (1994) *Freedom to Learn* (3rd edn), Columbus, OH: Merrill/Macmillan.
Rowland, S. (2000) *The Enquiring University Teacher*, Buckingham: Open University Press/ McGraw-Hill Education.
Ryan, J. and Sackrey, C. (1984) *Strangers in Paradise: Academics from the Working Class*, Cambridge, MA: South End Press.
Schön, D. (1987) *Educating the Reflective Practitioner*, San Francisco: Jossey-Bass.
Strathern, M. (2000) 'The tyranny of transparency', *British Educational Research Journal*, 26(3): 309–321.
Thomas, D. R. (2006) 'A general inductive approach for analyzing qualitative evaluation data', *American Journal of Evaluation*, 27(1): 1–10.
University of Otago Teaching and Learning Plan. Available at: http://hedc.otago.ac.nz/ tlp/introb.do?cms=public_access.los.otago.ac.nz (accessed 3 August 2010).
Van Manen, M. (1995) 'On the epistemology of reflective practice', *Teachers and Teaching: theory and practice*, 1(1): 33–50.
Wyatt, J. F. (1982) 'Karl Jaspers' The idea of the university: an existentialist argument for an institution concerned with freedom', *Studies in Higher Education*, 7(1): 21–34.

Index

Note: page numbers in **bold** refer to figures and tables.

abortion 90, 92, 95, 97
academic cultures 5, 34, 37, 49
academic freedom 7, 33–4, 62–3, 66–7, 84, 86
academic integrity 16
academic practice 35
academic traditions 31, 55
academic values 6, 31, 33–4, 52, 63–4
academics: attitudes to teaching 44; conflict between research and teaching 25, 27; conformism among 2, 5, 53, 99–101; identity of 25, 47; public 7, 82, 86, 99; role of in neoliberal era 66; training of *see* higher education, learning to teach in; values of 8, 28–9
accountability 7, 25, 60, 65, 67, 87, 98–9
assessment tasks 45
audit 66, 87
Australia 7, 65, 87
authority, culture of 49
autonomy 7, 28, 66–7, 88, 94–5, 98

behaviour, theories of 30, 35
biases 12, 33, 48
bioethics 93–4
Bloom, Allan 1, 86, 100

characterization 117
cheating 14, 42
collegiality 67–8, 99
course design 43–5
creativity 27, 43, 47, 98
curriculum, hidden 45

democracy 1, 27, 43, 55, 57, 84, 99
Dewey, John 51

disciplines, values of 6, 12, 29, 31
diversity 10, 63

economic freedom 65
Education Amendment Act (NZ) 85
empathy 117
empowerment 59, 85, 89
epistemology 25, 35
ethical dilemmas 6, 93, 116
ethics, teaching 95–6
expert, notion of 4, 102, 108

faith 38, 57–8, 60
feminism 54, 57, 60, 90–1
foundationalism 4, 10–11, 45, 52

graduateness 41
ground rules 52, 55–7

higher education: alternative organization of 48; and being critical 84–6; exclusion from 86; expansion of 62; foundational values of 3–4, 13, 15–16, 23, 27, 32, 42, 89; knowledge project of 16, 27, 67, 85, 88; learning to teach in 4–5, 13, 23, 26, 28; in neoliberal era 7–8, 64–9, 87, 89, 98; purpose of 5–7, 16, 62, 100; students' experience of 14, 43, 69; teaching in 41; values paradox of 64; values structures in **67**, **68**

ideology 7–8, 12–14, 48, 65–8
individualism 7, 42, 68, 98
indoctrination 4, 39, 51–2, 98
innovation 25, 61, 98
inquiry courses 46–8, 97

intellectual freedom 78, 88
intellectual honesty 13, 63–4
intellectual property 68–9

knowledge: controversial 29; disciplinary 11, 28, 41, 43; expansion of 66, 69; liberal ideal of 46; objective 12, 15; tacit 32; value of 13–14, 26, 28, 83, 88, 99
knowledge creation 26, 111
knowledge economy 25, 66, 68, 88

learners, good 27, 44, 48
learning: environment 15, 42, 48; motivations for 68; outcomes 45; skills 43
liberal traditions 46, 68, 83, 85, 88–9

McNiff, Jean 11
meta-narratives 39, 57
meta-thinking 14
methodology 35
mission statements 4, 34, 62–3, 97
morals 13, 48, 51, 60, 81, 85, 98–9
Morrison, Toni 5, 49

narrative inquiry 2, 112, 114–18
New Zealand 2, 7, 14, 47, 65–6, 85, 87

objectivity 13, 31
ontology 26, 35, 68

pedagogical relationship *see* teacher-student relationship
Performance-based Research Funding (PBRF) 66
plagiarism 14, 17, 19–20, 22, 32, 34, 42, 45, 52
practice, theories of *see* behaviour, theories of
practitioner-action research 35
professional ethics 95
professional learning 2, 5, 25, 28–30, 35, 116
professional life 15, 35, 97, 100

qualitative methods 2, 113–14, 117

rationality, technical 13, 53
Readings, Bill 109
reforms, neoliberal *see* higher education, in neoliberal era
relativism 4, 10–11, 45

research: accountability 66, 87; autonomy of 88; disciplinary 47; ethical choices in 6; funding of 69; priorities for academics 26
Research Assessment Exercise (RAE) 66
risk aversion 87

scholar, concept of 16
Schön, Donald 30–1
self-actualization 14, 46
self-inquiry 14–15, 23, 25, 31, 40, 50, 97
social change 33, 83
social freedom 84
supervision 28, 50, 95

teacher-student relationship 15, 26–28, 48
teachers, personal development of 44
teaching: content of 40; devaluation of 25; epistemology of 35; organization of 47; supervision of 50; values inherent in *see* higher education, values foundation of
tertiary education, use of phrase 65
thinking, critical 4–5, 10, 26–7, 41, 43, 45–6, 63, 99
tolerance 27, 39, 56–7, 83
transferable skills 28
transmission culture 47, 49
tutorials 46, 48–50, 88, 97

universities: public 6–7, 65–7, 98, 100 *see also* higher education
University of Otago: academic values of 63; Charter of 33; Teaching Plan 33

value conversations 1, 29
value decisions 9–10, 14, 29, 44, 49, 113
value judgements 12, 14, 27, 32, 38, 42, 97
value-resistance 101
values: contradictions in 53; defending 53, 98; ethical 14, 34; examination of one's own *see* self-inquiry; explicit 29, 45; imposition of 34; institutional 84; living 50; and morals 14, 51, 60, 85, 98; and ontology 35; in practice 13, 30; tacit 45; and academic tradition *see* academic values
values conflicts 52, 68, 98
values conversations 5, 32, 64
values decisions 41–2, 44
values narratives 3, 16–23, 36–9, 53, 55, 57–8, 60, 69–76, 78–9, 81–2, 89–90, 92–6, 101–2, 105–6, 111

values pluralism 11
values research 5, 59
values teaching: content of 42, **42–3**; explicitness of 50, 98; interactive 45; knowledge in 23; legitimization of 50; meaning of 9; necessity of 2, 5–6, 15; opposition to 11–14; and role modelling 97–8; special events in 46; styles of 32; theories of 31
values thinking 30–1

ALSO AVAILABLE

The Routledge Doctoral Student's Companion
Getting to Grips with Research in Education and the Social Sciences

Edited by **Pat Thomson** and **Melanie Walker**

This book addresses a set of interlocking and overlapping big questions that 'sit' behind the plethora of doctoral advice texts and run through the practice of knowledge/identity work.

April 2010: 246 x 174: 440pp
Hb: 978-0-415-48411-4
Pb: 978-0-415-48412-1

The Routledge Doctoral Supervisor's Companion
Supporting Effective Research in Education and the Social Sciences

Edited by **Melanie Walker** and **Pat Thomson**

This book places at its centre the interwoven questions of what it means to be a doctoral student in the social sciences, what is involved in becoming and being a researcher and clearly shows how the role of the supervisor is key to the student's personal development.

April 2010: 246 x 174: 360pp
Hb: 978-0-415-48413-8
Pb: 978-0-415-48414-5

www.routledge.com/education

Routledge International Handbooks of Education Series

The Routledge International Handbook of Higher Education

Edited by
Malcolm Tight,
Ka Ho Mok,
Jeroen Huisman and
Christopher Morphew

This volume is a detailed and up-to-date reference work providing an authoritative overview of the main issues in higher education around the world today. Consisting of newly commissioned chapters and impressive journal articles, it surveys the state of the discipline and includes the examination and discussion of emerging, controversial and cutting edge areas.

2009: 254 x 178: 544pp
Hb: 978-0-415-43264-1

For more information on this title and to order, please visit:

www.routledge.com/education